**HOW I NAILED IT
BY LEIGHTON DENNY**

ABOUT THE AUTHOR

Leighton Denny MBE is a multi award-winning entrepreneur, leading expert and internationally recognised figure within the beauty world.

Leighton left Bradford 15 years ago with just a dream and a rucksack and was awarded a Member of the Order of the British Empire (MBE) in the 2014 Queen's Birthday honours for his services to the nail and beauty industry.

With over 60 industry awards under his belt, Leighton is one of the best-selling expert presenters on QVC home shopping channel, achieving anything around £5,000 per minute for new launches. Somewhere around the globe, Leighton sells a crystal nail file every 15 seconds and a bottle of nail colour every 30 seconds.

Leighton's products are stocked in over 400 prestigious spas across the UK, over 1000 spas and salons throughout the world, and most recently in his first US salon in Washington DC. Ironically, Leighton is also stocked on the same cruise liner that he was once frog-marched off as a teenager.

Alongside his successful Expert Nail range, Leighton masterminded the launch of his premium self-tanning range, Sun Believable Expert Tan. Leighton added Lip Dual Expert Make Up to his expanding beauty portfolio just a year later and has recently launched his first fragrance, Light & Dark. Leighton has homes in London, Los Angeles and Bradford.

www.leightondenny.com
Twitter: @Leighton_Denny

CONTENTS

Prologue: St. Tropez, Summer 2002
1: Early life and strife
2: The house that Jack built
3: Fake it until you make it
4: Damned if I did, damned if I didn't
5: The school does nothing for Leighton
6: Secrets & lies
7: The anonymous letter
8: Cruising for a bruising
9: The great escape
10: Facing the fear
11: You only fail when you stop trying to succeed
12: The sweet smell of success
13: My encounter with Simon Cowell
14: Scales can only define your weight, not who you are
15: Jade Jagger and the key to Ibiza
16: Welcome to Harrods
17: Adding Spice to my life
18: The good, the bad and the diva
19: Don't follow your dreams, chase them
20: Lights, Camera and QVC

PROLOGUE

St. Tropez, Summer 2002

Celebrities loved me, the media loved me and all of a sudden I was THE man of the moment. I may sound a bit arrogant but at that point in time I felt pretty untouchable and was just running with my newfound fame and success. I'd achieved my dream of launching my Central London nail salon in Marylebone, and everyone wanted a piece of me. I was being featured in all the A-list glossy magazines and had earned a bit of a reputation so it wasn't long before TV production companies started pulling me in for loads of screen tests. I auditioned for everything from *Queer Eye for the Straight Guy* to *Love on a Saturday Night*. I was really gutted when I didn't get the presenting job for the dating show, *Love on a Saturday Night*. I'd got down to the final two but they chose Jonathan Wilkes over me. I always suspected it was because he was best friends with Robbie Williams. There were lots of things I didn't get that people don't know about as I don't usually talk about my failures. I just focus on my successes. But, believe me, there were a lot more failures than there were successes.

I was in my salon when I got the call asking whether I'd like to be in a new fly-on-the-wall TV show called *St. Tropez Summer*. The researcher for the show had remembered me from another casting call and thought I'd be perfect. There was no payment but it was a fantastic opportunity to allow cameras to film me in St.

Tropez over the summer for four weeks. I didn't need much convincing as I'd already bought into the lifestyle and was virtually packing my suitcase by the time I'd hung up the phone. St. Tropez is the playground of the rich and famous, and I totally believed the hype about myself.

Around this time, Tara Newley and I had become really good friends and were socialising quite a bit. My trip to film the show was perfect timing as Tara was going to be out there at the same time and we could hook up. Tara invited me to lunch at Club 55 in St. Tropez with her mum Joan Collins, who was also a client, and Joan's new husband Percy. Everyone was ordering salad, but I stayed true to my northern roots and ordered a portion of chips or fries as they call them in St. Tropez, darling. You can take the boy out of Bradford but you can't take Bradford out of the boy. Joan was horrified: 'Fries and salad? How absurd!' Tara just shook her head and said, 'Oh Mum, leave him alone. If he wants to have fries and salad, he can have fries and salad!' Joan and Percy hadn't been married very long so they were very touchy-feely. A lot of people were clocking our table so they were probably enjoying the attention too. It was crazy for me as I was sat having lunch in St. Tropez with Joan Collins! Club 55 was amazing and Joan goes there every day for lunch when she's spending the summer in St. Tropez. While we were there, I spotted Bruce Willis, Julia Roberts and P. Diddy. Everyone goes there – but I mean people I know from London and New York, not people from home in Yorkshire.

After lunch, we went back to Joan's villa so I could give her a manicure. She didn't allow any filming there but she was happy for the cameras to film me going to the appointment and en route back to the hotel after. Joan's hideaway villa is tucked away in a secret location. There's only one taxi driver who knows where it is. I've never seen anything like it in my life. It's exactly how you'd imagine a movie star's mansion to be – especially the swimming pool on stilts on the edge of the cliff. I did Joan's nails – in the summer Joan usually has red nails and in the winter she has a French manicure, but most people do it the other way round. Then we had some drinks and ended up playing Scrabble. It's crazy when you think I've actually played Scrabble with Joan Collins. Can you believe it? Leighton from Bradford and Joan Collins from Dynasty. It was me and Tara against Joan and Percy. They won and they were a little too good. I think they're Scrabble professionals and had definitely played once or twice before. It wasn't the easiest game for me to play but I never let on why.

Filming the fly-on-the-wall show was really good fun. My episode also featured Boy George, Ivana Trump and a posh London socialite who owned a cosmetic clinic in Harley Street. I got on really well with the production team so they started finding things to film me doing like hooking up with some rich kids holidaying at Nikki Beach. At Nikki Beach you can only sit by the pool if you're drinking Champagne. I'd brought my cousin Nancy out for a week to work as my assistant so we went and did all their nails. It was £90-£120 for a manicure in London but it was £235 in St. Tropez. That summer, everyone was going mad for crystals on their toes.
Having Nancy as my partner in crime meant the show could film us sunbathing and shopping, which is how I spent most of my days out there. I was going into really

exclusive boutiques and literally buying everything they had available in my size even though I couldn't really afford it. I was obsessed with designer clothes and I guess I was living the dream as they say! It was incredible and I loved the lifestyle – especially the yacht parties. The Champagne flowed and they were full of glamorous barefoot people. There would be a pile of Jimmy Choos in a corner as no shoes were allowed on deck.

I'd been staying in the Moroccan room at the Bliss hotel, an amazing boutique hotel with just eight rooms. I remember it had the most gorgeous fabric wallpaper, but luxury came at a price. That price was £10,000 to be exact. Needless to say I had to move to a cheaper hotel in the St. Tropez Port after two weeks as the cost was just spiralling about of control. But I was stupidly just living the lifestyle and absolutely loving it.

The most surreal day was the reaction I got when I was out shopping with Tara one day. A crowd of people started pointing and staring. At first, I thought it was just because they'd recognised Tara. But after awhile a couple of teenagers came up and asked for my autograph. In my head I was thinking, 'What the hell do they want my autograph for?' For a laugh, I just scribbled something down on the scrap of paper. I'd been in a few magazines but that was back home in the UK and, even so, I was hardly considered a celebrity. People started taking pictures of us and I heard someone giggling about Eminem and pointing at me. Then it twigged. They thought I was Eminem. Can you imagine? Crowds of people were asking for my autograph and I was just signing whatever they gave me - napkins, cigarette packets, the lot. In hindsight, I was really ripped back then, had the perfect eight-pack, was decked out in the latest designer clothes, sunglasses and of course, the tattoos! It all made sense especially as I was being followed by TV cameras. Well at least I know who could play me in the film of my life!

It was the most amazing summer ever and it all felt too good to be true - probably because it was. But I'll never forget the moment I went to the cash machine and couldn't get any money out. I was skint – totally skint. I'd spent thousands living the life, blowing ridiculous amounts of cash on Cristal Champagne and partying in the best nightclubs in the South of France. I'd totally bled my account dry. Revlon had sponsored me initially but that deal had run out, my own money had run out and the sad truth is I just couldn't afford to be there. So I was left with no choice but to cut the trip short and come back to London with my tail between my legs. Talk about coming down to earth with a bump.

St. Tropez proved to be my wake up call. I was starting to lose my direction and I did for a good couple of years. I was turning into the person people thought I was and that wasn't me or what I was about at all. Luckily I got my head screwed on pretty sharpish when *St. Tropez Summer* came on E4 that November. I hated the person I was watching on screen. I really regretted taking part in it even though I guess at the time it was one of the first reality TV series. I'd been edited to look like a right luvvie and I wasn't in the slightest. At one point, I was walking along the harbour near Ivana Trump's yacht and said something like, 'I really like Ivana and my people are speaking to her people.' I couldn't believe it when I watched it back, I was cringing. Worst still, it was one of those programmes that they constantly repeated so I felt there was no escaping it. Back then, E4 was a brand new channel and everyone was tuning in to it because it was on Freeview. Oh and the best bit? I was described as a self-made millionaire even though the production crew had watched in embarrassment as my card had been declined that day and they'd had to lend me money to get home.

I realised reality TV wasn't the right direction for me. I actually sat down with my mum and dad and explained if I became a Z-list star I would only have a short career and it could be damaging to what I really wanted to do. I quickly realised that all those people had short-lived careers and I'd already been working for a decade at this stage. I didn't want to become a celebrity as that wasn't me and I wasn't impressed by that life. So, I wound my neck back in to knuckle down and focus on what I really wanted to be – a true expert in the beauty industry.

1. EARLY LIFE AND STRIFE

My earliest childhood memory is of the hot sun beating down on my neck as I drive around our back garden in Bradford in my pedal car wearing my favourite red shorts and a white vest. It's 1977 and, back then, summers are like mini heat waves. I remember the day like it's yesterday because it's the first time I try to run away from home. I am three years old. I am forever trying to escape and I have no idea why. I was the baby of the family and the apple of my dad's eye, but from as early as I can remember I always wanted to get away and be free. I was crazy about cars and my obsession obviously started at an early age as I had a collection of pedal cars: an ambulance, fire engine and a sports car. I would spend hours speeding – well, as fast as my legs could run underneath – around in the garden!

All of a sudden I got the urge to escape. The only thing between me and freedom was our 5ft garden fence. My mind started racing as an idea popped into my head. I would balance all the cars on top of each other to stage my escape. So, with all my might, I piled the pedal cars on top of each other and scrabbled to the top by climbing up the windows until I was high enough to throw myself over the fence. I was fearless and so excited that my plan had worked that I didn't think about the 5ft drop on the other side. I ended up winding myself when I landed in a heap on the cold pavement. Ouch. Quick as a flash, I jumped up and started running as fast as I could because I was finally free. I ran around the house and onto the main street but as I ran across the road a car screeched towards me clipping the back of my ankle and throwing me face down onto the tarmac. I remember hearing the woman driver screaming and crying as this little figure had come out of nowhere and just run out in the road in front of her. It all happened so quickly so, in hindsight, she probably thought she'd killed me. The neighbour who lived in the corner house had heard the commotion. She ran outside, picked me up from the street and ran into her house to lay me on her sofa. I couldn't understand what was going on and what all the fuss was about. News travelled fast in our area and my aunty Tricia, who was Mum's sister, and my nanny, ran past the front window and into the house shortly after. Mum arrived just minutes later in a right panic. They bundled me up and off we went to the doctors. He gave me the once over and put an elastic bandage on my ankle, even though I probably didn't need one but at least it made me feel like a real patient. It's funny how you never forget your first brush with death and, believe me, there've been many brushes along the way. This time, I'd been very lucky to escape with just a few scratches and bruises but Mum had obviously called Dad at work and filled him in. He rushed home that night but he was shocked to find me happy as Larry jumping around the living room with my little bandage still on. He shook his head and said to Mum, 'There's nowt wrong with him!'

Mum and dad always had a great relationship and are still together over 45 years later. As a child, I always remember how solid they were even though I've never, to this day, really seen my parents kiss. They were never that affectionate towards one another in front of us unless they'd had a couple of drinks down the pub and even then it was only a peck on the cheek. That was it! Stuff like that is a bit taboo in our family. We always give loads of affection to our dogs and young kids but not towards one another.

It was a real love story between my parents as they first set eyes on each other in December 1960 but didn't actually start dating until Christmas Day 1963 when Dad had just come back from Germany where he'd been posted in the Army. The Army wasn't his first career choice. Dad was desperate to be a professional footballer, and he actually got onto the reserve team for Leeds United. But it wasn't meant to be. He injured himself in his second game so he went into the Army to train the football teams.

During the time Dad was in Germany, Mum had got involved in an abusive relationship. They'd had a child, my sister Amanda, and she was pregnant with my brother Stephen. Most of Mum's sisters were in abusive relationships where they were beaten regularly so sadly it had become the norm. Mum must have felt trapped with one child and another on the way but Dad proved to be her hero. When he came back he told Mum how he felt about her and vowed to look after her. Dad warned off her boyfriend and told him that if he ever stepped foot near my mum again there'd be trouble. No one messed with my dad. He was the strong, silent type who always kept his word. From that moment on, Dad swept in and took responsibility for Amanda and Stephen, just like they were his own. Mum and Dad finally tied the knot on 13 January 1971.

I was, by all accounts, a miracle baby when I was born in

May 1974. Amanda and Stephen are only 12 months apart, but shortly after Stephen was born Mum was diagnosed with womb cancer. She was told she wouldn't be able to have any more biological children which must have been devastating - especially for Dad. But eight years later Mum and Dad couldn't believe that she'd defied the odds and actually got pregnant. The doctors warned her that it was an incredibly dangerous pregnancy but she had no idea what was coming next. Mum had to stay in the hospital from three months pregnant until I was seven weeks old! Poor Mum was confined to bed rest. She had to keep her legs slightly raised the entire time as I was in a breech position – head up in the womb – which can cause huge complications at birth. Doctors hoped I would turn naturally if her legs were raised but it wasn't going to happen and she ended up having a caesarean section. They called me the miracle baby in that ward because in that day and age, with the technology they had, they couldn't explain how on earth my mum had fallen pregnant with a damaged womb. It just goes to show, nothing was going to stop me from coming. Whenever I was naughty Mum used to joke, 'From the moment I found out about you, you've persecuted me!'

Mum wanted to name me David Denny but Dad got in into his head that he would name me Leighton after two of his favourite sportsmen – darts player Leighton Reese and footballer player Leighton James. Not many people realise that Leighton is actually a Welsh name. As they couldn't agree on my name, Dad secretly registered me Leighton Jack Denny at the town hall behind Mum's back one day. She told me she went mental when she found out what he'd done. The joke is, to this day, Dad only calls me by my initials LD, and he'd only call me Leighton when I was in trouble. Everyone else calls me Leights which is ironic as I was always late for everything! Dad never treated me different even though I was his only biological child. We were always his family and he would do anything for us. To this day, I don't think Dad actually realises that we all know the truth – not that it matters, he'll always have three children in his eyes and that will never change.

Mum and Dad brought us all up with strong family values which they both shared even though my parents' backgrounds couldn't be more different. Mum – Margaret Patricia Veronica Denny – was from a huge English traveller family who'd settled in Skipton. She was the eldest of nine children but there were only seven surviving. She had five sisters – Sylvia, Patricia, Angela, Josephine, and Maureen – and one brother, Kenneth. One sister had been born stillborn and one brother had only lived for a month as he had a hole in his heart. My grandparents decided to donate his body to medical research as there was such little information about the condition at that time and it was quite a huge deal as he was one of the first to be donated. By the time I came along, my grandmother Margaret - Mum was named after her as it's customary that the first born children are named after their parents in travelling families – had moved from the caravan into a house. I remember it being decorated in lots of brass and full of horseshoes which is part of the travellers' rich heritage. My grandma had actually been born in a traditional green bow topped wagon – the ones that were attached to a horse – as it was common for travellers to be born at home in those times. My grandma always wore thick knit cardigans and

15

lots of jewellery. She'd wear sovereign chains and lots of rings. Grandma Margaret definitely dressed like a woman of her age and was definitely more homely than glamorous. My granddad Kenneth had a horse and cart and used to sell fruit and veg from it. He died of cancer when I was a baby but mum tells me he'd nicknamed me Marmalade because of the orange flecks in my hair.

Mum was a local beauty queen and she'd got to the finals of Miss Talk of Yorkshire, Bradford's equivalent of Miss World, a couple of times. She had the biggest blonde beehive, just like Marge Simpson, and a tiny little figure so it's no surprise my dad fell for her. She was definitely one of those natural beauties who didn't need much make up and would only wear it if she was going out. Mum still had that traveller mentality of getting red carpet ready with full on make up for nights out. She would always have a new outfit and I rarely saw her wear the same outfit twice. Mum would get ready with all her sisters when they were going out and it would be absolute mayhem. One of my aunties used to come round with bags of new clothes every Friday and I'd never suspected anything was dodgy until a few years later when she was sent to prison for shoplifting – on more than one occasion. Mum and her sisters were all glamorous but they were definitely a force to be reckoned with so if you messed with one, you were asking for trouble. I was a typical little boy and just thought my mum was the most beautiful woman in the world – as did my dad.

From what I can remember Aunty Josie and Mum were the closest out of all the sisters when I was growing up. Aunty Josie's husband Kevin was nicknamed Mad Dog

Riley and was one of the hardest men in Bradford. Everyone was terrified of him – even the police! They'd called him Mad Dog after he was involved in a brawl one night where someone had axed him in the back of the head. To split up the fight the police had set a dog on him. The dog bit him and he bit the dog back and the police and everyone called him Mad Dog Riley ever since.

I can relate to *Big Fat Gypsy Wedding* from my youth more than I can relate to anything else. Family parties, weddings and christening would always finish with men fighting in the car park or some family feud coming to fruition. But I wouldn't change anything about my past as it's made me who I am today and it keeps me grounded as I can appreciate all walks of life. I know what I should have had so that makes me thankful for what I have. I always knew I was going to do something different from the others even though I completely embraced the travellers' lifestyle when I was younger. I ended up wearing sovereigns and grew my hair into a mullet so I could fit in with that side of my family but the majority of them rejected me as they thought I was posh because I went to school.

I never really had a close relationship with my Dad's - Jack Denny – side of the family until later in life but we'd see them at family events. They lived in Horsforth in Leeds and were more upmarket than Mum's traveller family. Dad's mum, Nana Annie, had a complicated life and she liked a tipple. I sometimes got the feeling she wasn't very welcome at family events as she'd got a bit old and sour but I didn't care as she absolutely adored me. My parents were only in their thirties when I was born so they'd go out most weekends and I'd go to stay with Nana Annie. She owned a row of four terraced houses on the Bowling Back Lane and she'd converted the two middle ones into a greasy spoon café. She lived right opposite the travellers' site so I'd often bump into my cousins and other relatives from Mum's side of the family in the café. She lived in one of the end houses and granddad Richard lived in the other end house. I always thought he was Dad's real dad but only found out years later that he wasn't. Family secrets always seem to come out eventually.

Nana Annie was definitely a glam-ma back in her day. She used to wear Butler and Wilson-type costume jewellery and big fake fur coats with lion's or tiger's heads printed on the back. She'd made her money, bought property and definitely used to throw her weight around a bit. Although she owned the whole house, she only ever lived in one room and it was jam packed with a bed and sofa. A tiny back passage was the makeshift kitchen and she hardly ever went upstairs but that's where she would store all her clothes and fur coat collection. She was always dead glamorous when she was going out but when she wasn't she was the complete opposite and looked like a homeless person. She'd have stains down her as she had all those animals. Her house would always smell a little as all the animals lived in the same room with her! Nana had a big German Shepherd dog called Prince and two parrots – a McCaw called Sammy and a little green bird called Freddy – and they could both talk. They used to say, 'Where's me Jack?' referring to Dad. Sammy used to live in an old people's home so he used to mimic what they used to say like, 'I've pissed myself, I pissed myself.' I used to love it. Funny thing is after 10 years we realised Freddy was actually a girl – after 'he' laid an egg one day! Nana loved animals and also had two little lovebirds. It was so sad because for as long as I can remember Prince always had a lump on his foot. It ended up being cancer but I didn't know that. One day he just disappeared and no one had the heart to tell me he was dead - they'd told me he'd run away. It's funny as every time I see a medium or a psychic they tell me that I have a German Shepherd by my side with a big lump on its foot.

I loved spending the weekends there as Nana used to make the steam-in-the-tin treacle sponges, which were amazing, but I always remember that she used to cough a lot from all the smoking. She smoked a hell of a lot – around 60 Woodbines a day – and had an ashtray that was overflowing with cigarette butts. She only seemed to empty it when she couldn't physically fit another butt in there. Sadly she passed away from emphysema when I was 19 so I guess the cigarettes ended up killing her.

Dad has always been fiercely private but I know he must have had a tough time growing up as he'd moved in with Nana's sister, his aunty Audrey and her husband Doug when he was younger. Dad had three brothers: Harry had been knocked down and killed by a bus when he was six years old and Billy and Dennis had been adopted. But despite any issues he ever had with her, Nana Annie was still his mum and every night without fail he'd bring her her tea. I remember my mum putting aside an extra portion each day for Nana after she'd cooked our tea – which means dinner up north. We'd have breakfast, dinner and tea, unlike London where tea usually means a brew with jam and scones. All the same, it was pretty decent of Mum as they never really saw eye to eye and had more than a few cross words over the years.

2. THE HOUSE THAT JACK BUILT

We lived in a big, white detached house on Brookfoot
Avenue in Bradford and it was pretty impressive by
anyone's standards as it was the house that my Dad,
Jack Denny, built. That was Dad through and through, a
real grafter. You don't realise what a big deal it is when
you're growing up, but not many people can say that
their dad actually built their family home. It was a big
house and bizarrely I can still remember the layout even
though I was only small. Dad's always been a real
inspiration. In fact, both my parents are as they were
always self-employed and worked hard to provide for us.
Mum and Dad always worked together for as long as I
can remember. Dad was a builder by trade but he
worked as a TV engineer, which kept him busy as he
used to place ads in our local paper for his business.
Mum would book all his appointments and juggle looking
after the house. I'll give Mum her dues as she always
cooked our tea every evening and boy can she make a
mean Sunday roast, which is why I still love Sunday
roasts so much up to this day. Mum pretty much had a
weekly menu so every Monday we'd have stewing steak
with dumplings, Tuesday it was corned beef hash and so
on. Fridays we'd always have steak and chips or fish and
chips, so safe to say, Mum was definitely a bit Shirley
Valentine and liked routine. When she couldn't be
bothered it would be beans on toast. Although I had a
major bone to pick with her when I realised that she'd
tricked me for most of my childhood. I always thought
she'd cooked Cornish Pasties from scratch – until one

day I found the wrappers at the bottom of the bin. I imagined her like Bree Van De Kamp from *Desperate Housewives* slaving over a hot stove all day and she was just sticking it in the bloody microwave!

I was quite entrepreneurial, even at a young age. I was always thinking of ways to make money, whether it were by doing chores or dancing for cash. Mum and Dad were really sociable even though now they'll swear blind that they never went to parties. They'd go to the pubs, stay for a lock-in, go to the casino and the party would end up back at our house. I'd wake up and everyone would be drunk so I'd pretend to do robotics and go round with a glass collecting 50p off their friends. It was all robotic dancing during that time and everyone would cheer and clap. Aunty Tricia would always be with them as she came to live with us when I was quite young. She was like my second mum and as I stood there dancing in my little vest and pants she would proudly tell her friends, 'This is my baby and I brought him up. He damaged my hip.' I was glued to her hip most of the day and now she has a permanent reminder. Sorry Aunty Tricia!

We were a really close family but I don't really remember much about my brother and sister when I was growing up mainly because of the big age gap between us. I always loved our Amanda but we didn't have much of a relationship until I was much older. She and Stephen took me out through duress as they were already eight and nine by the time I was born. By the time they were teenagers they certainly didn't want a little five-year-old hanging off their coat tails, especially as I'd tell Mum and Dad what they'd been up to. As soon as I ran through the front door I'd grass them up if they'd been smoking or swearing – or both. I was Dad's little ally and I didn't care that they hated me for it. Stephen especially resented me and continued to do bad things to me - although I never felt bullied as I'd always get him back. I used to wait until he was asleep, sneak into his room and stab him in his back with a metal Afro comb! I remember one time I threw bleach at him. I'd always wait until he was fast asleep before I got my revenge and he more than deserved it.

Stephen always did his best to get me in trouble and I was quite gullible when I was young, as I didn't know any better. It didn't help that I was in the bottom set at school and had real problems reading and writing. I was so excited when he taught me how to write my first word - c*nt. It was really easy to write, as it was all the same shape apart from the letter 't' at the end. I didn't even know what it meant. He'd told me to write it down and give it to the teacher the next day at school. I didn't realise I'd done anything wrong until the teacher slapped me across my face so hard that I heard a high-pitched ring in my ear. I was stunned. I actually thought my brain had exploded. My parents didn't hit me growing up and I only ever recall my dad slapping me once when I poured petrol on a bonfire and nearly set his car alight. I think he did it out of shock at my stupidity more than anything else. But getting slapped by a teacher in front of the entire class was different. I couldn't even speak. It all happened so quickly and I clutched my stinging red cheek in shock before I got marched off to the headmaster's office for a proper telling off. Back then teachers could get away with doing things like that and they were the actual bullies, not the kids at school. I didn't tell my parents as I didn't want to get into any more trouble and the headmaster certainly didn't call them because he knew what the teacher had done was wrong.

I hated school and school hated me. But Dad was the one person who believed in me – even when the teachers didn't. He would try his best to encourage me to learn by teaching me a new word on the way to school. There'd be interesting words like 'sapling' and he used to teach me loads even though it was hard for me to remember. We'd do a different word every week and every day we'd talk about that word and spell it so I understood its meaning. Dad always thought I'd be a footballer. Rain or shine, he'd come and watch me play whether I had a game after school or even on the weekends. Truth is, I never wanted to be a footballer but I wanted to make Dad proud. I'd do owt to please Dad but I just couldn't control my behaviour. By the time I got to Tong Upper School I still hadn't read a book and I could just about recognise words from the Rainbow Books from primary school. You could get away with it in those days. Some days I'd turn up for lessons without a pen and just sit there. The teacher's way of dealing with it was just to ignore me. So while everyone thought I was unruly I was just disruptive to hide the fact that I couldn't do what the other kids could do. If a teacher said, 'If I hear another pip out of any of you, that's it!' I'd shout out 'pip' as I couldn't help it. I couldn't read and write and the only way I could mask it was to be the class troublemaker and get kicked out of class every day.

It probably didn't help that I was late for school every day without fail as my parents were always running late. It was a mad rush every morning and we'd grab breakfast from the caravan by the side of the motorway on the way to school. Dad would buy me a boiled hamburger with tomato sauce, a bottle of Irn-Bru fizzy pop and a packet of Seabrook cheese and onion crinkle cut crisps. No wonder I ended up being a little fatty! Dad always took me and collected me from school in his faithful white Ford Escort estate. If he couldn't make it back to pick us up, he'd send one of his workmen. Dad knew trouble started before and after school as that's where you could get waylaid so he made sure there was no danger of that.

Business was booming for Dad at that time and he opened a shop called Sureview TV's in a huge rented building on Tong Street, a major road running from Bradford to Leeds, as everyone was renting TV's. It was a four-storey property with a massive shop, basement for storing the TV's and a two storey flat where we ended up living. The shop was on the edge of two council estates, Holme Wood and Bierley. Dad always managed to get us private houses but they were always bordering council estates. It gave me the edge to want to better myself but all my friends and babysitters lived on the council estate. Dad had also bought a plot of land in Bierley where he started building another family house that we'd eventually move into. He was a hard worker and great role model who always set such high standards being self-employed. Dad also set the most amazing example for us to strive for. Myself and our Amanda are more successful than Dad ever dreamt of being. As for my brother, he's just a big disappointment and ended up in the gutter. It just shows you can have a bad egg as we were all given exactly the same opportunities.

I was always more frightened of Mum growing up as even though Dad was strict he'd spoil me. Looking back, it was probably his army background which made him that way. We used to have bottles of fizzy pop delivered to the house every Friday and Dad would religiously mark on the bottles how much we were allowed to drink in one day. One gorgeous sunny day I'd been called in to have my tea and I was desperate to get back outside and play so I was rushing my food. Dad knew exactly what I was up to so he made me chew each mouthful fifty times. But Dad was fair when he needed to be and he would make me do chores to get a reward. I'd wash the cars and cut the lawn in exchange for money. Dad felt by rewarding me he'd keep me from going down the criminal path. There were a lot of criminals around me and we had lots of family members who had never worked a day in their lives but Mum and Dad were different from the rest. They never had anything to do with any criminal activities and they were devastated when my older brother fell into that world. Even though it was around me they always made me understand that it was wrong. Sometimes people would bring stolen goods into his TV shop but, whereas some would turn a blind eye to it, Dad would never accept it and would always send them packing.

I tried my best to stay on the straight and narrow but as a kid you just want to be accepted and I ended up knocking around with kids from the Bierley Estate and travellers – like my best friend and cousin, who everyone called Gypsy Jim. Let's just say we would get into lots of skulduggery together - as everyone did at that age!

3. FAKE IT UNTIL YOU MAKE IT

I always knew I was different but I never really understood what made me different from the other boys. I spent a lot of my childhood in a state of confusion and trying to fit in with any peer group that would accept me. But one person who liked me because I was different from the other boys was my first girlfriend Sally Bell. We were both around 12 years old and she was the popular girl at school. She had short dark hair and was really well groomed. Dating in those days just meant holding hands, walking into school together and a few innocent kisses. It was more about being seen together and looking back it was more of a friendship than a relationship. Sally lived on Tong Street just down the road from our school and Dad's TV shop so we would rush back to her house every evening to watch our favourite TV programme, *Home and Away*. Dad would come and collect me from Sally's every evening.

Sally came from a nice family and they really liked me but I ended up having an affair with Maria. Maria was the older sister of a boy in my class. She was a little older than us and was really developed for her age. She was blonde with big boobs and my first sexual experience with a woman was with her. One night when she came round to babysit me and my cousins, she started kissing me on the sofa. One thing led to another and it went a little further than kissing – and I enjoyed it. I was completely obsessed with her but she ended up using me. The affair went on for a while and Maria used me to buy her things in town whether it was a blouse from Mark One or shoes from Jonathan James shoe shop. She'd always say we'd go out later and hang out but she'd never turn up and just leave me standing on the street corner for hours. I'd let her do it to me time after time. Sally's best friends Annette and Leanne saw me out with Maria one day in Wakefield and reported back. I'd lied to Sally about where I was going so she dumped me and that was our relationship over with.

Looking back I really struggled with my sexuality and I don't even remember when I first realised I was gay as I tried so hard to fight it. The only gay man I was aware of in our town was the one who owned the hairdressers and would drag up on the weekends. He was a Kissagram drag queen and that's what I thought being gay meant. I knew I didn't want to be like him so I was really confused. Back then there were no gay people on TV like there is now. What's strange is at school they'd tease me for being gay. The kids would run around shouting: 'Leighton's gay! Leighton's gay!' I think they teased me because I was different to the other boys. I had white blonde hair, was always immaculately groomed and my best friend, Suzanne Blamires, was a girl. The teachers were no better than the kids and I remember one of them saying to me in front of the entire class, 'Oh Leighton, you're so gay.' I'd stand up and just turn the table over which meant I'd get into even more trouble. They would constantly provoke me and I'd fall for it each and every time. It was a real time of confusion for me as I really fancied Sally and liked kissing her but deep down I knew I had to be with girls to make Mum and Dad happy. Being different wasn't acceptable and my parents definitely wouldn't like it.

Funnily enough, all the signs had been there all along. I loved Madonna and the first CD I'd ever bought was *Like a Virgin*. I'd gone into WH Smith in the town centre and bought a pencil with a rubber on the top, a pencil sharpener and the CD. I also had a *True Blue* poster up in my bedroom. Madonna sang about all the things people didn't talk about. She was just so out there and I loved how she wasn't afraid to sing about what she wanted or wear outrageous clothes and be as daring as she wanted to be. I couldn't get enough of her. I even loved her film *Desperately Seeking Susan*.

Curled up on the sofa watching TV with Mum was one of my favourite things in the world. I'd lay there with my head on her lap as she played with my hair until I fell asleep. We'd watch all those fabulous American TV shows together and I loved their lifestyles as it seemed so removed from mine. They were all beautiful, drove sports cars and I always used to think that I wanted that life one day. I was obsessed with the shows and used to say to Mum, 'I wish we'd been born in Beverly Hills. I really wish I'd been born into that life.' My mum turned to me and said, 'Just because you weren't born in Beverly Hills doesn't mean you can't pretend you were. Just remember, you fake it until you make it.'

Maybe I'm guilty of faking it and pretending I was just a normal lad who was into girls when deep down I knew I was very different. But I put on a good front and no one had any reason to suspect otherwise. I played the role of the perfect younger brother and I was proud as punch walking into church as a pageboy on the day of Amanda's wedding. I was 12 years old when our

Amanda got married for the first time. She was only 21 and had a church wedding that afternoon and a party at a club that night to mark her milestone birthday. I was decked out in my immaculate suit and it was yet another event to remind me that I had to put those confusing thoughts out of my head. Lads were supposed to get girlfriends, get married and start a family. It was my sister's first marriage to a lovely guy called Neil. Amanda had my niece Nicola quite quickly after getting married and moved back home when Nicola was just 18 months old as sadly things didn't work out with Neil. Amanda's since moved on and is now happily married. Nicola and I have always been really close as we grew up together more like brother and sister. Nicola was a gorgeous baby and I loved teaching how to do naughty stuff when she was old enough. I was quite a hands-on uncle or as much as I could be for my age. Our Amanda was always a bit dubious about leaving me with Nicola as I always wanted to take her out and show her off to my friends. I adored her and still do, and now Nicola's had a daughter, Brooke, I adore her too. It's like a reincarnation and it's lovely to see the generations come together.

Around this time, I had my most memorable holiday when Mum and Dad took me to America. We always went to Europe so it was such a big treat for us to venture so far but I think the real reason we went was because my parents wanted to take me to Disneyworld before I grew out of things like that which came quite soon after. They actually had to force me to go away on holiday with them after this trip. Back then the pound was really strong against the dollar and I remember Mum going into a baby boutique in Florida called Sarah-Louise and buying almost everything in the shop for my niece.

We were all so excited about a new addition to the family and Mum was beside herself about becoming a grandma. She went crazy and bought everything from dresses and bonnets to booties and cute bottles. The whole trip was such an eye-opener as we flew to Orlando and did Disneyworld, Epcot Centre and Universal Studios before driving to Miami on the infamous I-95 highway. Dad was always good at getting bargains and when we arrived in Miami he'd got us a great deal on a room at the Fountain Bleu Hilton on Collins Avenue. It was an amazing hotel full of old people. But we couldn't care less as it was the most gorgeous hotel we'd ever stayed in.

One night, Dad overheard someone talking about us in German at the bar. He'd been based in Germany and his stepdad was German, so Dad was fluent in the language. He turned round in a rage and said something back to the man in German, which obviously took this guy by surprise. Dad ended up arm wrestling this guy in the middle of the hotel bar while all the other holidaymakers looked on. Dad won, of course. He was such a strong man and no one messed with him. He wasn't a violent man or a fighter but people knew not to mess with him. He was the best dad ever. It's tough now as he's had three strokes and rounds of chemotherapy and radiotherapy to treat cancer. Unfortunately, he's started to lose his hearing now so, depending on the environment, it's hard for him to even hold a conversation these days. But he's still here and that's all that matters.

It's strange how there were subliminal messages all through my early years about my career path but I've never really made the connection until now. The America trip was one of those light bulb moments. Mum used to be a terrible nail biter and would bite her nails down until they were half way down the nail bed. All her sisters did it too and it was worse when she felt nervous. But when we went to Miami she decided to get her nails done in a salon for the first time. I went with her and really enjoyed watching the process happen. I sat there transfixed as I saw the nail technicians applying acrylics to other customers, and it really stuck in my mind. At that stage they were doing nail art and nails were such a big thing in America. Mum had pink and white acrylics that looked like natural nails but people were having rhinestones applied and all sorts of cool designs. All the women in the salon had really long nails and were even doing airbrushing and spraying designs on. This was another experience with nails that had been planted. It just goes to show that if you listen to your destiny there are messages there to pick up on. I ignored the messages for a long time and when I eventually listened and acted on it my career took off. When I think back, I feel like I was always destined to follow this path.

4. DAMNED IF I DID AND DAMNED IF I DIDN'T

By the time I was eleven, Dad had opened Denny's Wine Bar in Keighley. It was a busy wine bar, business was booming and I used to cash up the tills – even at that young age. I'd been working in Dad's businesses since I was a kid so I'd worked my way up from being a glass collector to cashing up and paying the staff. Dad hired Billy, who was 19 at the time, to be one of the doorman and also my security. The bar had hundreds of customers so we took a lot of money every weekend. Billy lived near the bar in Keighley so I'd stay over at his parents' house on Friday and Saturday night then go back home on Sunday with the takings. I was actually running the bar by the time I was 13. I didn't have many close friends as I still struggled to find a group I belonged in but everything changed when Billy came along. We started spending a lot of time together and developed a really close friendship.

I was definitely a chip off the old Denny block. I looked years older than I actually was and never dressed like a teenager. I always like to dress smartly and would wear a different shirt and tie each day. My dad always taught me if I looked the part, people would think I was the part. He also said dressing smart was a sign of good manners and it showed respect. Dad told me not to worry about my reading and writing as that would come later. I just had to look like I could do it and people would believe I could. Being advanced for my age and very streetwise, I always wanted to do what the older kids were doing so I convinced Billy to come on a Club 18-30 holiday with me to Corfu – to celebrate my 14th birthday! No one even questioned that I was underage as I was so mature. Mum and Aunty Josie were going to Corfu over the same fortnight so that was why I was allowed to jet off to a foreign country with my best friend in tow. When we arrived, the apartment in Kavos was pretty basic. Bearing in mind it was a Club 18-30 holiday, it probably wasn't even a two star. But I loved the freedom of hanging out with Billy for two whole weeks. We looked quite similar and people just assumed we were brothers so no one ever questioned what sort of relationship or friendship we had. We just clicked because we understood each other. There was never anything intimate between us but our relationship was very similar to *Beautiful Thing* and I could definitely identify with that film when it came out. It's a beautiful story of a pair of teenagers growing up in a similar working class background to me and how they'd become aware of their sexuality. They're confused when their casual closeness eventually awakens their sexual feelings. They are unsure of what to do as they are only vaguely aware that they're gay. It felt exactly the same with me and Billy. Neither of us knew another gay person so we knew we had feelings for each other but we didn't think we were gay either.

We celebrated my 14th birthday on one of those all-inclusive boat trips where you can eat as much BBQ food and drink as humanly possible. We drank beer non-stop and got absolutely wasted. It was so much fun, but a few days later I saw Billy's jealous side. We were both drunk again and this time he turned violent. A guy had walked into the bar wearing tight cycling shorts where you could see the outline of his manhood and I glanced over briefly and giggled. He flew into a rage so I ran out onto the street. He followed me and attacked me, giving me a black eye. He was an amateur boxer and he probably had a bit of brain damage as he had a twitch in his right eye, but boy did he have a lethal right hook. The bottom line is we were just stupid kids and he wasn't very bright. From that moment, I saw a different side to him and didn't like it one bit. The mild mannered, caring Billy had disappeared and it scared me.

By day five of our two week holiday we'd run out of money after being totally robbed by the 18-30 reps who'd encouraged us to book all trips and meals in advance. We supposedly had a trip every other day, signed up for everything going on our first day and they basically robbed us to death. We'd splashed the cash in excitement and were left totally broke so we had no other option but to hire mopeds to drive to where Mum was staying with Aunty Josie a couple of villages away to get some more money. I wasn't old enough to hire a bike so I changed the date on my passport from 1974 to 1970. Back then we had hand written passports but little did I know that would be the same passport that landed me in trouble years later. When we reached the village Mum was staying at she was shocked when she saw I had a black eye but I just told her we'd got drunk and I'd bumped into the wardrobe. Aunty Josie wasn't buying my story though and kept asking, 'Did Billy do that to you? Did he? Tell us.' I said, 'No, no, no.' They knew he was a boxer and had put two and two together but I refused to admit the truth to them as I wanted to protect him and, more importantly, protect our special friendship.

That was the night I got stabbed. We'd all been out to dinner – Mum, Aunty Josie, my little cousin Jolene and her best friend Nicola, and me and Billy – at a lively Greek taverna where they'd been smashing plates. It was really good fun and we'd had a great time. We were on our way back to the apartment and these guys on motorbikes started circling around us. It was really scary as it was quite dark and Billy and I were the only guys in our group. Then this guy got off his bike and started trying to pick a fight with Billy for no reason. We had women and small children with us but they didn't care. They started to fight. I jumped in to try and stop it and got stabbed in the back of my arm. Luckily, the police came out of nowhere and arrived just in time to arrest the guys, as they definitely would have robbed us had Billy not been with us. They were local troublemakers and in those days you had to be so careful as there were no streetlights. You'd go out for dinner at 7pm but it would be pitch black by the time you were heading home at 11pm and there were always loads of power cuts in the Mediterranean back then. The joke is I hadn't even realised I'd been stabbed and I've still got the scar on the back of my arm to prove it. They took me to hospital and I got four stitches. Stuff like that was just part of the course back then. I'd seen people have their noses bitten off in my dad's wine bar. Women used to fight more than men and because I was a glass collector I saw a lot of people getting glassed. I was also an inquisitive kid so when things did kick off I didn't run behind the bar, I watched everything. Sadly, the fight took the edge off the holiday and Billy's pride was bruised as this guy had knocked him out just as the police arrived. Mum was really frightened for me and Billy. She gave us some money and made us go back to Kavos as she didn't want to risk these guys coming back to find us. When we went back to our apartment we wound it in and didn't touch a drop of drink for the rest of the holiday.

Me and Billy continued our close friendship back at home
and carried on working at Denny's Wine Bar after my
aunty Tricia and her husband Gary bought it from my
parents. Things took a nasty turn when Billy persuaded
me to start giving him free drinks during his shifts. He
used to drink pints of lager when he was paying but I'd
got into the habit of slipping him Jack Daniel's and Coke.
I hated deceiving my family by stealing drinks from them
and, worst still, he was drinking on duty. Aunty Tricia
caught us one day and we all fell out which really upset
me as she and I always had such a close bond but I
ruined it all because I was so naïve.
We both left Denny's and got a job in Berlin's wine bar in
Bradford. Even though I was still underage, Dad's friend
Walter managed the bar and he knew I was a brilliant
barman. Dad had trained me up so I was a really handy
person as I knew how to do all the jobs from collecting
the glasses to serving behind the bar, changing the
barrel, cleaning the pumps, collecting the money on the
door and standing in for the DJ - I could do it all. It wasn't
long before I was slipping Billy free drinks again and the
alcohol would fuel his jealous streak.

Some older friends from school came in once and I was
on my break having a laugh with them. He got really
jealous and ended up throwing them out and getting me
by the throat by the fire escape. It frightened me that
things could get out of hand. Billy and I had done nothing
wrong but if people assumed we were gay, our life as we
knew it would be over. I'd found out what had happened
to some people who were gay in Bradford. It was looked
upon as a lifestyle choice and not that you were born that

way. It was around the same time Elton John came out as gay. Although Elton had revealed he was attracted to both men and women back in the 1970s, it wasn't until 1987 that he came out as gay in *Rolling Stone* and it made headline news. I remember being in the car with Dad once and something about Elton came on the radio. Dad turned to me and said, 'You make sure you stay away from men like that. It's disgusting. I remember thinking, 'Oh God.' I knew his feelings on the subject. He said, 'It's not normal.' He said it with such disgust. I knew I couldn't ever come out to Mum and Dad or even tell them that I suspected I might be different. Thinking back now, I don't think Billy really cared about me. Maybe I was just a naïve teenager and he was just using me. I loved spending time with him and really cared about him as he'd convinced me we could get a place together when I was old enough.

With both our wages, we were on about £300 a week which was pretty good money for teenagers. We saved our money in a pot at a woman called Yvonne's house. She was obsessed with boxers – especially Muhammad Ali – and took a real liking to Billy as he had won a few titles at this stage so was getting well known in the area. We used to hang out with her all the time and her home became a safe haven for us. We were really careful as we had to keep our friendship a secret outside of work so I'd dial Billy from a pay phone and hang up so he could call me back. We'd arrange to meet at the cinema and sit in the back row and just hold hands.

We had a regular routine where I would stay at his house on Friday and Saturday night. He would always be in the bath when I got to his house and he'd ask me to wash his back. It was all so innocent but I knew people wouldn't approve of our friendship if they knew about it. Every Sunday, we'd work for Billy's dad who owned a civil engineering company. We'd help him dig holes in the road for other companies like British Gas to lay pipes. It was £50 per day cash in hand and we needed all the money we could get to save up for our place.

Billy was Irish and I'll never forget his dad catching us in bed on St Patrick's Day, which is obviously a big day in any Irish household. We'd gone out on the Saturday after work and come back drunk. We'd been chatting on Billy's bed and I'd fallen asleep with my arm around him. It was all very innocent but his dad had come in to wake us up that morning. I remember him screaming in a thick Irish accent, 'What's going on? What's going on? Get him out of here now! He's never allowed in this house again.' They must have had their suspicions that he was gay, as we'd done nothing wrong. He had bunk beds and I'd forgot to get into my own bed that night but his dad didn't care and banned me from seeing Billy ever again.

Keighley was like no man's land for us so Billy would come and stay at our house occasionally. The sad thing is Billy really couldn't control his temper and kept flying into those jealous rages over the silliest things. Although it scared me at the same time it was exciting. I'd seen my aunties and uncles and cousins behave like that so it was just normal that there was always a dominant figure in a relationship. After my uncle beat my aunty to a pulp once she had to have her ears sewn back on. Mum and Dad were never violent towards each other but I'd seen it happen around me. It was a regular thing. But I was actually more scared of people assuming we were gay than I was of him hurting me. One time he marched me out of the bar's fire exit and had me by the throat. I'd been giving him free drinks so he was drunk and that's when his temper always came out. He was telling me he'd seen me flirting with some customers and I should stay away from them or there'd be trouble.

I'd had enough and I couldn't cope with the roller coaster of emotions. I ran round to the front of the wine bar where there was a taxi rank and screamed that I wanted to go home but I didn't have any money to pay for my fare. He grabbed a fist full of pound coins out of his pocket and threw them aggressively in my face. The hard coins smacked against my cold face. Scraping a few coins off the street, I jumped in a taxi and cried all the way home. When I got home I told my dad I didn't want to work in Berlin's anymore and I didn't want Billy staying over either. Billy came back to our house not long after and I overheard him telling dad that I was just a stupid kid. He packed up his stuff and left our house but that wasn't the end of it. He used to call me on the house phone but as soon as I'd hear his voice I'd hang up.

You couldn't be gay back then as it was too dangerous. I'd heard stories about these infamous brothers in Bradford who'd abused a guy they suspected was gay with a snooker cue. The hairdresser who used to drag up was really feminine and I didn't want to be like that. I really didn't think I was gay and Billy didn't think he was either. He'd get offended and say, 'I'm not f**king gay.' I was so confused and realised I was between a rock and a hard place with my sexuality as I was damned if I did and damned if I didn't. So, I felt it was time to get a girlfriend again and go back to faking it as it was safer.

5. THE SCHOOL DOES NOTHING FOR LEIGHTON

I had matured a lot faster than the average kid so despite only being a teenager I felt like an adult and was treated like one. I always wanted to be older from a young age and I've always had big ideas. I set up my first business when I was 14. My sister had bought a load of fancy dress costumes from a car boot sale but she lost interest in setting up a hire business. So I took the costumes off her hands and decided to do it myself. The first year, I ran it from Mum and Dad's house and put an advert in the local Bradford newspaper, The Telegraph & Argus, advertising costumes for hire. It was a seasonal thing as I'd mainly hire them out at Halloween and over the Christmas season when people used to throw fancy dress parties on New Year's Eve. As soon as I realised I was onto something, I hired my sister's mother-in-law Pam, who was a dressmaker, to make me more costumes. I'd worked out that I'd pay Pam £8 to make each costume so it paid for itself the first time I hired it out, that way I'd make a quick profit. That was me all over. I wasn't book smart but I was street smart and I was good at making money. The more money I made, the more it motivated me.

Being savvy, I didn't waste time on capitalising on my newfound success and got myself a full-page feature in the local paper. I told the reporter that it was my dream to make lots of money and buy Mum and Dad a house, which I'm proud to say I've been able to do now. I also wanted a Ferrari and a private jet and all those things that you later realise aren't obtainable when you're old enough to know better. But I was definitely impressed by all those expensive material things like everyone I knew in Bradford was. Funnily enough, I actually remember telling the reporter that I wanted to be a jeweller when I grew up. Jewellery used to be a big part of our life. My mum would wear lots of chains and sovereign earrings, and even though we'd moved away from the travellers' style we still had that look. I used to wear a lot of sovereigns and I actually got mugged in town when I was out with Sally Bell one day. The guy snatched it from my neck but I was determined not to go down without a fight so I chased after him. I actually got hold of him but let him go when he pulled out a knife.

I ploughed all my energies into my fancy dress business and it proved to be an instant success. I was raking in so much cash that I didn't need to do any other part time work when it was closed at certain times of the year. I was saving up my money to buy a car as it was always about getting a set of wheels. I wanted a White XR3i convertible with a black soft-top roof. As the business got busier, Dad suggested I move it into a corner of his TV shop so it could be open all the time. Mum worked from 9am-1pm and I worked from 1pm-5pm so we were able to man both businesses, which worked perfectly for us. Just a year later the costume hire was a full time business and I employed schoolmates to work for me after school paying them £1 an hour to put flyers on cars. Property developers had bought a derelict piece of land opposite Dad's TV shop and had completely regenerated the area. They'd opened a Superdrug, Iceland and Nettos, which made the footfall passing our business go crazy. We had more customers than ever. One Christmas and New Year, I was all out of costumes even though I had over 3,000 at this stage. I lost interest with the business when I was 16 and sold it to buy my XR3i convertible. I advertised it in the local newspaper and sold it to a couple for £15,000. Although I did keep one of the costumes for a memento – a Teenage Mutant Ninja Turtle one – which is still in my parents garage to this day!

I definitely inherited Dad's business sense but thankfully I didn't pick up on all his bad habits – apart from a cheeky bit of gambling. He was always a bit of a gambler and couldn't resist putting some money on the horses and dogs or sometimes having a gamble down the casino. I was addicted to the fruit machines in Dad's wine bar and would spend all my money playing them every day. Dad thought of an ingenious way to solve my addiction – he bought me my own fruit machine for my bedroom! That way he could show me how much money I was actually gambling away each day. This is what I loved about my dad; he always explained things in a simple fashion so I could understand the error of my ways.

My siblings and I never went without anything – ever. But don't get me wrong as we used to earn our money and I've probably washed my dad's car more times that I've ever washed my own. Dad trained us a bit like he did the dogs. We had to work for our treats before he gave us treats. He wasn't tight but he was frugal. He always taught us to shop around and I think that's why I was so frivolous when I started earning money. Although we never wanted for anything, we didn't always get what we necessarily wanted.

Once I got to upper school, the only thing I ever really

wanted was a pair of Nike Air Max trainers which were the must-have trainers. At the moment, I must have about 30 pairs and I think it's a bit of a psychological thing for me now. Even if I'm not sure I really like them I buy them just in case. Back then they were still super expensive and I was desperate for a pair of white ones with big multi- coloured laces and Nike written in big letters around the heel. I was like the guy in *Charlie and the Chocolate Factory*. I would catch the bus into town to go to Sports Shoes Unlimited just to look at the Nike Air Max. I'd even go when the shop was closed as I could see them from the shop window. Dad would never let me have them as he said they were too expensive for a pair of trainers. Instead he used to get me Dunlop with the Velcro straps. Don't get me wrong as they would always be a nice substitute pair but they just weren't the ones I'd set my heart on. I remember showing him a pair of trainers in the shop that I really wanted and he took a pair of my old ones and sprayed them a different colour to look like the ones I wanted. I loved them but when I wore them to school the kids teased me. Needless to say, as soon as I started earning money the first thing I treated myself to was a pair of brand new Nike Air Max and it felt like all my Christmases had come at once. I wore them until water started seeping into the soles, I just couldn't bear the thought of binning them.

Throwing myself into work with the fancy dress business and working at Dad's TV shop part time had been the perfect distraction from all my confusing thoughts around Billy. We went from being super close to not having any contact, which was hard, but when I cut someone off I do it for good. I didn't like the person he was becoming and felt that the only way I could protect myself was to sever

46

all ties with him as he'd become really controlling. Once our friendship was over I actually started to go to school more often as Billy used to encourage me to bunk off. I didn't really need an excuse to skip classes as I hated school anyway. I still couldn't read or write that well but by this time me and Suzanne Blamires were thick as thieves and were forever causing trouble wherever we went. We were playing truant from school one day when we went to Halifax and got our first tattoos. We both got red devils – she had one on her boob and I had one on my arm. Suzanne had even dragged along her mate Rachel who was a Jehovah Witness and she got a devil on her boob too! We didn't have much cash at the time. We got red devils done as that was the only tattoo we could afford. We were just young and stupid. It bloody hurt and tattoos hurt no matter what anyone says. I ended up covering my red devil with a black panther years later as I thought it looked tacky.

I had no business getting a tattoo so young but, again, I wasn't your average 14-year-old. Scared that Mum and Dad would hit the roof, I pretended it was just a transfer for the longest while. I thought I'd got away with it until we went on holiday a few months later. I remember my dad saying, 'Funny how you're sweating through that transfer LD!' My dad absolutely hated tattoos as my brother was covered in them. But Stephen had horrible tattoos like 'love' and 'hate' on his knuckles and swallows on his neck. They definitely weren't designer tattoos like everyone has today. That was the beginning of my obsession with tattoos. It's funny how it took David Beckham coming on the scene years later to make tattoos really popular. On the London clubbing scene tattoos became a big thing as everyone was taking their tops off and showing off their bodies. I got my last tattoo done about 10 years ago and I regret having them done now. I'm seriously thinking of getting them removed one of these days. I think I fell into that mindset where I was trying to look more masculine. When I was younger little kids used to ask me, 'Are you a boy or girl?' People used to tell me I was a little bit too pretty to be a boy. I guess that's probably another reason why the kids called me gay at school.

I got expelled from school a few months before my 15th birthday for fighting. The headmaster told my dad, 'The school does nothing for Leighton and Leighton does nothing for the school.' When Dad used to drop me off to school every morning he'd say, 'Please don't make me come back to school today.' I never even made it to lunchtime before I was calling him to come and collect me as I'd got into trouble again. There was a pay phone in the sixth form area so as soon as I got in trouble I'd run to the phone and call my dad. School was relentless as older kids would always try to bully me but I wouldn't have it, no matter how hard they tried. They'd push me and I'd push them back. Dad always taught us to face the fear. One day, as a little kid, I had run into the house because an older kid had hit me. My dad calmly opened the front door and made me go back outside and hit him back. He said, 'No, I'm not coming to tell them off. You're going to have to go back out there and hit that kid back.' And from that moment onwards, I always hit back.

I hated most subjects, and towards the end of my time at school I would only go to drama classes because I really got on with the drama teacher Mr Bullock. Drama was a form of escapism for me and it was the only subject I actually enjoyed. But the rest of the time Suzanne and me would be getting in trouble and spending our lunch hours in detention. The most ridiculous incident happened in the deputy headmaster's office when he actually volunteered to fight me. I kid you not. He took off his jacket and squared up to me, saying, 'Come on then, if you think you're hard.' I had balls but I certainly wasn't about to get into a scrap with my deputy headmaster even though now I realise that he was probably just trying to frighten me.

After I'd been kicked out of school Dad refused to let me off the hook with my studies and he hired a private tutor to teach me Maths and English after I'd been expelled. I'm dyslexic so that didn't help as I found it hard to concentrate. I would have probably been diagnosed if it was today but you weren't during that time. I was just classed as a naughty kid who was disruptive in class. I think the private tutor tried to explain to my dad that I had some form of learning difficulties but my dad wouldn't hear of it, which in hindsight was probably a massive oversight. There was a real lack of understanding of things like this in my day. You were either bright or a dunce. I would lose interest half way through a page of a book. I found it really hard to read and I still do today. I still can't spell very well. My dad bought me a computer called Speak and Spell when I was younger and I also used to have a little machine by the Franklin Mint Company where I could enter a word and it would tell me what the correct spelling and meaning was. I could rely on that and I would always have it with me. Later down the line, Dad sent me on a computer course called Sight and Sound Education at the Yorkshire Evening Post building in Leeds. It had been recommended to my dad by my private tutor and it taught me a lot as it was visual. As well as helping me with my reading and writing it also taught me how to type and use a PC. Dad would always say, 'You need to learn computers LD'. As always Dad was right - computers were the way forward.

Once I left school I started working full time at my Dad's shop but would still hang around with Suzanne who was at college training to be a nurse. She became a really close confidant who I could share my deepest, darkest fears and secrets with. I confided in Suzanne that I suspected I was gay and she loved it. She loved anyone who was different especially as her family was so diverse. She told me she fancied a lesbian fling too. I don't think she was a lesbian but she just wanted to try anything. She had a real addictive personality. It was typical Suzanne as she was wild and loved anything left of centre. Suzanne's aunty was a lesbian so I started hitting the Nottingham gay scene with them which was a really interesting experience. I still wasn't confident enough to tell people that I thought I was gay, but I loved the freedom of hanging out with other likeminded people.

Suzanne was really wild and I'd heard on the grapevine that she got caught stealing medication from the hospital she was working at. That was Suzanne's problem, she always took it too far. Things took a turn for the worse when Suzanne started injecting speed. Her friend's brother was a bad 'un who had introduced her to hard drugs and she became a heroin addict.

By this time, Suzanne and I had lost contact. I went to her house once but her mum just slammed the door in my face and told me she didn't live there anymore. When

50

I did bump into her several years down the line she was so skinny and obviously ravaged by years of drug taking. She married the bad guy and just continued to go off the rails. It's so tragic as Suzanne became a prostitute and was murdered by serial killer Stephen Griffiths, who was infamously known as the Crossbow Cannibal. I was at home in London watching the news on TV when Suzanne's murder came on a few years ago. Suzanne had gone back to his home and it said on the news that when she'd tried to escape he'd killed her with a knife in her head and crossbow bolt in her back, before dragging her body back into his flat. Worse still, he'd chopped her up and police divers later found over eighty pieces of her body in the river. It was sickening.

Suzanne was his last victim and her murder had been caught on CCTV, which is how they finally caught him. A few days later, the caretaker at his block of flats came across the footage of Suzanne's murder when he was going through the CCTV tapes to find out who was responsible for vandalising the building with graffiti. I felt sick to the stomach and just couldn't believe it. I was stunned that someone I knew and spent so much time with had met such a gruesome end. I was so distraught I had to take some time off work as I just kept going over it in my head. The sad thing is Suzanne became world news, which is what she always wanted, but it was for the wrong reasons.

6. SECRETS & LIES

I've always been good at keeping secrets, and I remember one of the biggest ones I've ever kept is covering for my friend Tricia who would sneak out to meet her boyfriend.
It was all very cloak and dagger as she was dating a Muslim guy and in that day and age interracial relationships were frowned upon. It just wasn't accepted like it is today. Back then, we didn't know about their cultures and beliefs so they weren't accepted. Bradford has a small town mentality and if you don't know about something you just reject it.

That summer I'd been hanging out with one of my favourite cousins, Jolene. She's my aunty Josie's daughter. They lived opposite Walter and Jean who are Tricia's parents. I was about 16 and Tricia and her best mate Ayshia were a couple years older than me and were the coolest girls I knew. Tricia Branning was always dead ladylike and always had a full face of make up on.

We spent a lot of time in and out of each other's house as our parents used to socialise together a lot during those times. Aunty Josie and my mum thought Tricia and Ayshia were bad girls and they didn't really approve of me hanging around with them but I loved it. Ayshia and Tricia used to date guys from different races but I couldn't care less as the girls were fun and they'd take me out drinking all the time. Ayshia had been banned from driving but she used to nick her mum's car. She'd wait for her mum to leave the house then we'd all jump into her black sports car and go speeding around the town. It was wild.

At the time, I was working for Group 4 Security doing data input, which sounds more impressive that it actually was. The truth is I would just scan a package and press enter so it was logged into the depot. I used to work from 5pm to 9pm every night and I'd get a lift with the delivery drivers to Aunty Josie's and sometimes I'd stay over. Jolene would let me sleep in her bedroom and she'd bunk in with her mum. Jolene's bedroom window used to overlook Tricia's bedroom window. I remember going over to close the curtains and I spotted Tricia climbing out of the window and getting into a taxi with the guy she was dating. I didn't breathe a word to anyone but word eventually got out. It always did in close-knit communities. But Tricia was feisty and I knew nothing would stop her doing or dating who she wanted to. Little did we know that Tricia and her secret lover Yaser would one day become the parents of Zayn Malik who just happens to be a member of one of the biggest pop bands in the world – One Direction. It just goes to show what a small world it is and I'm so excited for Tricia that her son has become an international popstar. Maybe we were both sprinkled with a bit of success. Our summer of fun was cut short when Jolene grassed us up to Aunty Josie as we didn't let her hang out with us one afternoon. Tricia and Ayshia let me drink cider in the park and my aunty stormed over screaming, 'Ayshia! Tricia! I'm going to tell your mothers that you're letting Leighton drink and he's underage.' That was it, I wasn't allowed to go near them and we'd only bump into each other at family parties. The good thing about Bradford is there's a real sense of community and our families are still close to this day. It was so sad that Tricia's dad Walter died when Zayn was on the *X Factor*. We were all really fond of Walter and I know he would have been so proud of all Zayn's success. My aunty Josie still lives close to the family and often pops round with stew for Tricia's mum Jean. As for Ayshia, she was also studying to do nails at the time and still does my mum and sister's nails in Bradford.

Aunty Josie and my cousin Jolene were definitely part of the holiday crew with Mum and me. Mum and Dad could rarely go on holiday together because of the businesses so we'd all go instead. We usually went to Spain or the best deal we could get on Teletext. We used to go on holiday loads, probably about three times a year to places like Malta, Greece and then Turkey when it became the new in place.
It was all about cheap deals not like now where I've got a checklist of things to go through before I book my holidays. I'm obsessed with the little luxuries like room service, a pool and whether it's in the perfect location. Back then, it was all about cheap fun in the sun. My sister Amanda was working for Teletext so she'd find out deals before they went live and we'd quickly book them and get amazing deals.

The one time Mum and Dad decided to take a break together they left me to look after the TV shop and the dogs. Dad always had dogs as he trained and raced greyhounds so loads of dogs came into our lives. We had paddocks at the back of the house where Dad would walk them every morning, at lunchtime and again when he came home in the evening. Some Sundays the greyhounds would get proper cooked chicken breasts and would eat better than us! Dad was quite big on the greyhound racing circuit. It was more than a hobby for my dad as he ran it like a business. He'd take me to all the dog meetings and race nights and I used to walk them up and down in front of the bookies so the people got to see the dogs – like they do with the horses – then I'd put them into the traps.

The most greyhounds we had at any one time were four. Dad did NGRC (National Greyhound Racing Club) which is a licensed greyhound track where the dogs have to live at the track and he also raced some dogs on the unregulated flapping tracks. Sometimes it would be trials or a big race night and it was always really exciting. Dad would even take a few people down to place bets on his dogs. I was totally my dad's protégé and he taught me everything he knew about greyhound racing. As well as the greyhounds, I also had a pet dog called Major. My first dog Della was stolen after two days. I was devastated so Dad went back to the same litter and got Major who ended up being the best dog ever. He was my best friend and, like I said, we were always more affectionate to our animals and I loved him to the bone. Major was a guard dog but he was never vicious to us. We had him on a cattle chain so he could run around the house. He was a German Shepherd and really huge like a lion.

Funnily enough, dogs were the reason me and my brother had a huge altercation and I vowed not to speak to him again. Apart from the odd times he wormed his way back into our lives, I've had no contact with him for absolute years now. Back then, Stephen was going out with an ex-prostitute and they were taking heroin together so he was more screwed up than normal.

While my parents were away, I would feed the greyhounds and Major in the morning and walk them first thing. I was really conscientious and looked after everything for my dad while he was away. I'd close the TV shop around 4.30pm as we'd generally finish for the day when business got quiet. When my dad was away, I'd place ads in the local newspaper under the free ads section selling something different from the shop every day. I'd pretend it was a private sale or house clearance from my parents' home. I used my own initiative to do it as I thought it was an easy way to make a sale each day and get some money in. It also meant I could drop the RRP as I wasn't selling it directly from the shop. I could knock a fiver off stuff and it's amazing how well I did each day. That was me all over, a little wheeler and dealer always looking for ways to shift stock and make money.

The greyhounds earned dad money so we always had to ensure they got fed properly. I put the meat in the oven and went off to deliver a few items for a customer and install a TV and video. By the time I got back to the house it was late, almost 7pm. The greyhounds seemed a little bit irate out the back and I couldn't understand why. As I'd been busy with deliveries, I'd asked Stephen to take the meat out of the oven, mix it in with biscuit and feed them – that was it. Unfortunately, he hadn't fed the dogs so they were starving. We had four dogs at the time but as a couple were fighters, we had to keep them separated in pairs. Steven had got them mixed up and I could hear them going berserk in the back garden. I went out there with a bowl of food and one of the angry dogs attacked me. It was terrifying as they bit my hand so hard it was virtually hanging off with blood pouring out of it. I've never seen anything like it in my life and still have the scar. Somehow I managed to calm the dogs down and split up the fighters. The annoying thing is they'd already fought each other, which is bad for racing dogs as it knocks their confidence so they don't perform their best at races. I knew Dad had a big race coming up so I was really annoyed as the one thing I'd asked Stephen to do was feed the dogs, but this was my brother all over. He couldn't even take the meat out of the oven and feed the bleeding dogs! When he came in I said to him, 'You didn't feed the dogs!' He swore blind he did, so I asked him what he'd fed them with, as I'd found the meat still in the oven. He said he'd fed them and put another bowl of meat in the oven. Full of rage, Stephen went for me and we ended up having a full on fight in the garden. By this point I had my thumb all bandaged up from the dog bite and the blood started pouring out again. I was going out with a girl called Sonia who jumped in, as did Stephen's druggie girlfriend. I ended up throwing him out of the house. I said I'd never have anything to do with him again and I kept my word.

By this time, Stephen was 25 and had been in and out of prison about five times. He was always hanging around with villains and getting into trouble. He was usually arrested for drugs but what would be really pathetic is that he was always in and out of prison for petty theft like nicking CD players from cars. He'd robbed us all and was always nicking our mum's jewellery and selling it for quick cash. My dad would end up trawling the pawn shops to try and find it so he could buy it back. Stephen wouldn't care what he stole or how many times he broke my mum's heart. I used to find her in tears as he'd taken things that weren't necessarily worth a lot of money but had sentimental value because her grandmother and family members had left them to her. Worse still, he mostly stole from us rather than from strangers, as he knew we wouldn't call the police. He knew all our routines so it was easy to steal from us. We wouldn't prosecute him but then he'd end up getting involved with something else and end up back in prison. We wouldn't hear from him for a couple of weeks then all of a sudden Mum and Dad would get a letter asking for batteries, soap or a transistor radio. They would always send what he asked for and I'd always tell them that he'd never learn if they kept answering his letters and sending him stuff in prison. I told them to make it as difficult for him as possible in there but he was their son and they would always stand by him, regardless of what he did to them. Stephen was just a bad egg and whatever they did, and they tried every which way to help that boy, villains and drugs impressed him.

My dad always supported Stephen and even set him up with a ready-made business taking over from him to install TV aerials. He set him up with a van, all the equipment and even customers as Dad had decided he was getting too old to be climbing up onto roofs. He taught Stephen everything but after about four weeks he didn't come home one day and Dad heard that the van and the equipment had been sold. Stephen had done a runner again and gone off on a drug binge. It was like a cycle, he did the same thing all the time. Amanda was really clever and took a step back from it all to concentrate on her own life. Stephen was a lost cause as he'd been like that for as long as I could remember. I'd found injection needles and a burnt spoon in his bedroom once. He's a compulsive liar and would lie even when he didn't need to. I'd actually say he was a pathological liar, as he actually believed his own lies. We always had to watch our back as we didn't know what he would be up to from one day to the next.

I shouldn't have been surprised by his behaviour as this was the very same person who kidnapped me and injected me with speed. It was like a bad dream. Stephen wanted to ruin me and he wouldn't stop until he did. This was a major turning point for us all - especially my parents. I'd walked into our kitchen and caught Stephen and his friends injecting themselves. He'd left home by this stage and he'd broken into the back door but I'd come home early and caught them in the act. He was with two friends and they held me down. While I was screaming and trying to fight them off they injected me with speed. It was a nightmare and it happened over the space of three days as my parents were on a short break away. My life just turned upside down and I couldn't function. I hadn't opened Dad's shop, the dogs hadn't been fed on time and all Stephen wanted to do was ruin me so it got to Dad. I was such a conscientious little guy for my age. Bearing in mind that at 13 I was helping Dad manage the wine bar, at 15 I was going onto Dad's building sites and acting like his foreman making sure everyone was keeping to time constraints, and by 16 I was managing everything for my parents and they were going away on holiday together all the time.

After about three days, I woke up in a haze in a dingy flat in Holme Wood Council Estate. It was a drugs den. It was a ground floor flat in a high-rise block of flats and people were climbing in and out of the window rather than using the front door. If you took drugs in this guy's flat, you had to give him some. He wasn't very bright and was bullied by most of the people who came in and out. It was like a squat and was dark and dingy. He had this really strange washing machine that sat on the top of the kitchen counter. It was so disorienting waking up and looking around this horrific place. I looked around and realised that I didn't fit in. I was wearing a pair of black polyvelts with black trousers and a charcoal grey silk shirt. I was daddy's boy and I was dressed to do business. But when you've been injected that amount of times with speed and amphetamines things play with your head and I ended up thinking I quite liked it. I remember saying, 'Why have I never done this before?' but I was obviously off my head. I was actually thanking Stephen and asking him why he hadn't told me to do it before. Everyone was being friendly but I didn't want to be there anymore and whatever I'd been taking had run out. I climbed out the window and run all the way before anyone realised I was missing.

By the time my parents came back they knew something was up as my behaviour was different. I'd never really stayed out all night without telling them and all of a sudden Stephen and I became really close. When I got home that night I didn't want to go upstairs and wake Mum and Dad up so I stayed downstairs and ended up falling asleep on the rug in front of the fire. My parents had woken up and saw me asleep but they told me I'd jumped up and screamed, 'You can't get me!' and I said to Mum 'If you put potatoes on top of each other they turn into sausages.' So I was talking gibberish, running upstairs saying, 'Ha ha they won't get me!' before I ran back downstairs and fell back asleep. I don't remember any of this but I do recall waking up and realising the gas fire was off. I turned around to see my mum and dad sitting in silence staring at me. I felt normal and they were just firing questions at me, 'What have you been taking? Where have you been? Did someone put something in your drink? Think about it, there's something wrong with you.' I had this flip out moment I don't remember and then I ended up breaking down and telling them what had happened. They were horrified and the next day I was on a flight to Malta with them. I slept on a camp bed in the same room as my mum and dad and they just watched me sweating as I came off the drugs. I think they felt that they were putting me through rehab. I was so sorry that I fell into Stephen's trap and made them go through that horrible experience but it wasn't my fault.

We stayed in St Julian's Bay for about 10 days but the first few days were torture. I was waking up in cold sweats and felt dreadful. I lost about 10lbs in three days. No surprises but Stephen went missing for months after this, which was usually the case. But my parents finally realized that they could no longer support him as he'd crossed the line. But that wasn't the end of Stephen.

After we disowned him, he came back and burgled our house. I came home to find the front door bashed in and I remember instinctively grabbing the hairspray which Mum used to leave on the shelf in the hallway. I have no idea what sort of weapon that would have been to fight off burglars.... a can of bloody hairspray! When Mum came home she ran straight upstairs to check her jewellery and I heard her sobbing when she realised that this time everything was gone. She was devastated because she had quite a collection of jewellery as every time my dad had a win at the casino he'd buy mum some gorgeous pieces to treat her. I remember her saying, 'My jewellery's gone. My jewellery's gone.' Not only did he steal her jewellery but also all my clothes, the money from the fruit machine and Mum's prized Lladro collection – which were gorgeous figurines she'd got from Spain and had spent years collecting. We knew it was him because he was selling our stuff on the estate so my parents didn't bother pursuing it with the insurance company as it would have landed him in trouble with the police again. It's just such a shame as I don't think he'll ever realise or appreciate all the pain and anguish he caused our parents over the years and how every line etched on Mum's face is probably because of him.

7. THE ANONYMOUS LETTER

I passed my driving test on the first day I could legally drive – my 17th birthday! I passed first time mainly because I'd been driving for a while. A long while actually. I bought my XR3i and went off the rails partying like everyone was at that time. If you didn't there was something wrong with you. I'd sold the fancy dress business but had ended up forking out £10,000 for the car and £4,000 for insurance. It was daylight robbery. To make matters worse, I only had the car for six months before I wrote it off. I was on my way to Manchester and a foreign guy was turning right as I was overtaking. He caught me, swung me round and I ended up in a ditch. I was devastated. My car was beyond repair. I was gutted. I didn't get a penny as I could only afford third party cover. The guy pissed off back to France and I only got £1,000 for scrap – after I'd spent £14,000 on it with the insurance.

So I needed to make some money fast and ended up getting a job at Grattan catalogue stuffing envelopes with those offers and mail outs. I did that for a while before I got bored. Dead end jobs became my middle name as I desperately tried to find some sort of job that I half enjoyed. I was always hard working but just struggled to find the right thing to do. Amanda was now working at a recruitment agency so I was never short of temping jobs and that's how I ended up working as a forklift truck driver as she'd got a contract in for British Greeting Cards, a massive company that supplies all the greeting cards in England. They needed a bulk of people to do the job and would put you on a forklift truck driving course then give you a job at the end. I did the course with my sister's first husband Neil but we ended up getting jobs in different factories. It was amazing money as I was on £375 a week. I was saving up for a new car and ended up getting a little red Vauxhall Nova. I'd gone down a peg from my XR3i convertible. Driving the trucks was probably the first time I really got bullied. I worked with much older men and they wanted me to get a load of greeting cards on my forklift truck and throw them over the side of the security fence so a van could come and steal them. It didn't bother me that I was the youngest at most places where I worked as I was confident, a hard worker and wanted to be able to do everything, but I wasn't prepared to steal for anyone. The job didn't last long before I decided to move on.

I was even a hairdresser – for about a week! My aunty Carol let me come and work with her in her salon and let's just say I wasn't exactly what you'd call a natural. I remember doing a blow dry and got the woman's hair stuck in the back of the hairdryer and it actually had to be cut out of her hair. Another time I had a customer who came in with gorgeous long hair and I ended up putting perming solution on her hair twice instead of using the neutraliser. As I was taking her rollers out clumps of her hair were coming out too. It was so awful. So, it was a very short-lived career before I realised it wasn't for me.

My worst ever job was being inside the Wimpy man in Bradford town centre giving children hats and toys. I think the real reason I even entertained the idea was because I really liked Wimpy fish and chips – that was my real motive, the free food. I had a job behind the counter but for some reason they always wanted to put me into the Wimpy man with the silly big hat. But the free food and the cash was enough to make me stay for a while as it was hardly a glamorous job wearing that ridiculous outfit.

What's really bizarre is I got a job at Crestol – which later changed its name to Robert McBrides – which was another big warehouse in Bradford. And guess what I was moving around this time? Nail polish remover. It's funny that there were so many little signs along the way. I stayed there for a while but I quickly realised that forklift trucking wasn't going to be my desired career. I ended up working back at my dad's TV shop as it was something to do. By this time, things had got really complicated in my life as I was still dating Sonia and I still didn't want to accept that I was gay. My gay friends would tell me that I was gay but I would tell them I wasn't.

I had started hanging out with a guy called John who had a bit of a troubled past. He'd just come out of a children's home when we started socialising together. Things got messy when John sneaked Sonia into a gay club to try and prove to her that I was gay. She flipped out when she saw me in that environment and he'd convinced her that I was leading a secret life. John and I ended up falling out big time and we ended up scrapping in the street one night. The truth is I'd been on the gay scene for about three years but I never slept with anyone or did owt with anyone. I was petrified as they had all the HIV adverts with gravestones falling down and icebergs floating slowly through water. We still thought you could catch HIV from toilet seats at this stage. 'Don't Die of Ignorance' adverts were everywhere. They frightened me to death as I was still trying to accept my sexuality. I still didn't think that I was gay after everything I'd been through and most of all I didn't want to disappoint my family and friends.

When I was 18 someone sent an anonymous letter to my mum and dad telling them that I was gay. That letter changed my life forever and it was a really difficult time for me. The contents of the actual letter are a bit of a blur to be honest as I was too shell-shocked to take it all in. My parents said in disbelief, 'Have you seen this, Leighton? Look what someone's written about you. Do you have any idea who would do such a thing?' They didn't have a clue in the world and didn't even question the fact I could be gay. I took a deep breath and said, 'I think I might be.' My mum went absolutely crazy and later that day she started throwing towels away that I'd used while my dad thought I was just going through a stage. I didn't know what to do so I ended up moving in with John to get away from it all. My head was all over the place. At the time, John was just about to jet off to Miami with his wealthy boyfriend and they paid for me to go with them. It was a bit crazy as John wasn't a nice person. His boyfriend Granville was an ex-police officer and he'd got a massive pay out after something happened to him on duty. John was given a daily allowance and just getting money off him with all these terms and conditions. I suppose it was a bit like having a sugar daddy. Poor Granville thought he was having a relationship with John but the truth is John was just using him. It was a fun trip though and it was definitely an adventure which is what I needed after the whole episode with my parents. John and I met a family of florists from Manchester on the plane to Miami and we ended up getting really paralytic with them. I mean really drunk to the point that we were throwing up in sick bags. They were wild. We bumped into them on the plane home and the daughter was telling me how nail extensions were the next big thing. She'd been out to Miami to do some training as her mate in Manchester was charging £35 for a full set of nails and it only cost her £3 to do. It seemed like crazy money so I decided to get into nails.

By the time I got back home, Mum and Dad had sort of got over the bombshell letter. Mum was still a little bit off towards me but my dad tried to understand. They definitely thought I was going through a phase. I lived in Bradford so, although I couldn't understand it at the time, now I understand the way they reacted. I know what it's like in that town. It really is a small town mentality.

So I was back with a new plan and told my parents I wanted to do a course in nails at a college in Leeds. Mum said, 'What do you want to do that for? So everyone can start laughing at you?' Anything I showed a passion for my dad supported me to do it. As long as I was on the straight and narrow he didn't care what it was. Dad said, 'Yeah, no problem, we'll lend you the money to do the course.' I did the three-day course at the Leeds School of Nail Technology with a company called Creative Nail Design. They had a salon downstairs with a training room above and it was run by an American woman called Gigi Rouse. While I was doing the course I put an advert in the Telegraph & Argus advertising my services and from then on I went freelance –before the course had even finished. I was mobile, got fully booked and life was good. I charged £22.50 for a full set of nails, £15 for a fill in and £10 for a manicure. It was quite expensive for a freelancer but people knew I was good and recommended me to their friends. I was so busy and I was enjoying it as the money gave me a newfound independence. It meant I could get a better car, buy nice clothes and do all these things I wanted to do for myself.

Bradford clients were so diverse. I started off doing family and family friends but as I got better and better, word spread and I was working all the hours to keep up with all my new appointments. Before long, business took off in a big way and I ended up renovating the bedsit at the back of my dad's TV shop. We painted it all white, put down flooring and bought two computer tables from IKEA. My friend, who I used to go clubbing with, Mayling, was a qualified beauty therapist so she came and worked for me. As business took off, I expanded to most of my dad's TV shop. I had two fully booked sun beds, a fully booked beauty therapist and four fully booked nail technicians. I trained everyone to do things my way. Then I started doing some night beauty courses and even one in aromatherapy massage. They were short courses every Tuesday for 10 weeks. There was a new government initiative so the courses were free at a training centre in town.

As I became a success, I got an apartment in The Calls just off Call Lane in Leeds. It was THE address to have as it was on the river. It was £120 a week, which was expensive, but I didn't care. It was just a little apartment with an open plan kitchen and living room that I'd furnished with a cream sofa with blue piping. It had a staircase that led up to the bedroom and the bathroom. It was great for me to be living in The Calls and I'd picked it as it was so close to the Leeds gay scene. But I soon realised that I didn't actually want to be that close to the scene after all. I'd left home but I was still round for my tea every night as the salon was in Bradford and closer to my parents. I thought my new flat was going to give me more independence but I realised I didn't actually want the independence that I once desperately craved. I was only in my flat around 10 months before I decided I'd had enough. I realised I'd rather have the extra £120 a week in my pocket – and it was a hassle coping with all the bills as well. I moved back home shortly after Lady Diana died.

I'll never forget that fateful day she died. I was on holiday with my friend Joanne Taylor in Gran Canaria and we'd been out partying the same night she died. I'd woke up bright and early with a bit of a hangover so I thought I'd slip out of the apartment to catch some rays. As I went to the reception to get a towel, the guy behind the desk looked stunned and said to me, 'The Princess is dead, the princess is dead.' I said, 'Sorry, I don't know what you're talking about.' But he kept saying it over and over again, 'She's dead, the Princess is dead.' I fobbed him off and went down to the beach where I heard someone crying. They were talking to someone back home saying, 'Oh my God, Lady Diana, I can't believe it!' I just couldn't believe it and ran back to the apartment to wake Joanne up. We were both in complete shock and immediately rang home to speak to our mums. It was so weird as it felt like it was someone we knew or someone in our family who had died. My mum was sobbing down the phone and told me it was true and how she'd died in an awful car accident. All the bars and clubs in Gran Canaria closed that night out of respect so Joanne and I just went out for dinner. It was dead morbid as it was also our last night there. At the time, you got the newspapers the following day on the continent so we got up early the next morning to get them all. We just sat in the apartment reading them and reliving it all over again before we left for the airport. It was just really, really sad.

The morning of her funeral, I closed my salon in Bradford as a lot of businesses felt it was the respectful thing to do. As soon as the main part of the funeral had finished, I got in my car and drove from my apartment to the salon. It was Saturday afternoon and I never saw one car on my journey from Leeds to Bradford. There were no cars anywhere and it felt like the whole world had stood still for her. Lady Di was definitely one person I would have loved to have met. I always imagined that if she were alive today she would have been a client. She was so just stylish and had just the right amount of glamour and class, but was still very much a real person. What she represented and did for the landmines and HIV was astonishing and she touched so many people as she really did make a difference. My parents were never really royalists but my dad bought a full sheet of Princess Diana stamps after her death, framed them and they now have a proud place in our living room. It's quite morbid but he always tells me that he's leaving those stamps for me when he dies. I guess that's an interesting thing for me to look forward to. Thanks Dad!

8. CRUISING FOR A BRUISING

It's been the theme running through most of my life but I was getting itchy feet again and I felt like it was time to escape from Bradford...again. I'd been to a trade show in Manchester and spotted an advert in one of the free industry magazines for staff for a cruise ship. It sounded like fun so I sent off my application form. I never really expected to get called for an interview for Steiner, one of biggest companies that operate spas at sea, at their Grosvenor Street HQ in London. I couldn't believe it when I got the job! I felt like it was a fresh start for me so I was really excited about starting my training. We were based at a YMCA in Essex. They made us live like we would be living in the ships so there were two sets of bunk beds in each room. I guess it was a test to see if we could cope with the ship life. We commuted to London every day and the training I got prior to going on the cruise ships was the best training I've ever had in my whole career. Steiner Training Academy was excellent. I was trained by Ian Carmichael, who was the Queen's private hairdresser, and a woman called Penny. They really liked me so they spent some extra time with me. Years later, I met Ian's partner who worked at QVC and he told me that Ian always knew I'd make a name for myself. Imagine that, I'd got a glowing endorsement from the Queen's hairdresser.

I'd only done a week's training when a ship came up for me and I was jetting off to America for a new adventure. Mum and Dad picked me up from Essex and drove me to

Heathrow airport for my flight to Miami. Everything was so exciting and when I arrived in Miami they paid for me to stay in a hotel that night as the ship came in the next day. Even though I was on my own, I was excited about my new adventure and, it's funny, I never really used to get nervous. I wasn't the most intelligent person but I had bags of confidence. I've definitely got my parents to thank for that. I had the gift of the gab and could always talk the talk, even if I couldn't always walk the walk – but that came later.

Life on the cruise ship, MS Carnival Ecstasy, was AMAZING! I was confident doing manicures and pedicures but now I had experience in facials, make up application and even retail sales. When the salons on the ship were quiet we'd get passengers in and give them free mini facials. This is what gave me my first taste of the salon environment. Working on the ship was fantastic as Steiner had an incredible reputation and throughout my career I've always maintained those high standards.

This wasn't my first time on a cruise ship as I'd been on one with my mum before from Cyprus to Egypt and back, but this was a brand new ship and I hadn't seen anything like it. The best thing about it was I was the only man working with 19 women. It was like having 19 mothers and it was fantastic! They all looked after me and I became best friends with a girl from Essex called Tracy. Tracy from Essex, how ironic! She was a proper little Essex girl who really took to me and was forever saying 'awww babes' and giving me little squeezes. We both cried buckets when I got transferred onto a different ship just a month later. Apparently, I was never meant to stay on the MS Carnival Ecstasy, I was just there to build up my experience and training.

I was absolutely devastated when I got transferred onto the S.S. Norway. It was a really old ship and I hated it. I'd just been on the sexy new carnival cruise ship that had two mini cruises a week so the salon always had new customers. MS Carnival Ecstasy was brilliant as we had two lots of passengers a week so we were always busy. You've got to remember when you work in a salon on a ship you're only busy in the beginning of each cruise as everyone does all their treatments when they arrive on board. The rest of the time it's dead quiet.

It was rubbish pay as we only got £50 a week paid into our bank account at home. Tips were paid to us out there as well as a commission but everything on board was inclusive so we didn't pay for a thing. Even the crew bar was heavily discounted which we definitely took advantage of.

The MS Carnival Ecstasy had been brilliant as it went from Miami to Key West to Cozumel in Mexico and back to Miami. It was two three-day cruises a week then we were docked in Miami one day a week. The SS Norway was two week Caribbean cruises with lots of rules and regulations. Unlike the carnival ship, this one wasn't party, party, party anymore.

I'd just been on a brand new spanking ship but this one looked liked the Titanic and still had the big brown chimneys. The S.S. Norway was old, brown and just depressing. There was a place around the back of the ship that everyone called Slime Alley. Everyone would scrape the leftovers from their plates into this big bucket of slop, which was just disgusting. I couldn't eat the food as it was just slop. I remember telling my boss that I couldn't eat so I couldn't work. It didn't help that the salon director and spa director didn't like me. I was a bit unruly to be fair. I had my own cabin on the MS Carnival Ecstasy because men and women weren't allowed to share but I was sharing with three men on the S.S. Norway. When I walked into my cabin for the first time, I froze. It was absolutely disgusting and you couldn't see the floor for all the pizza boxes and Pringle tins that were scattered everywhere. I refused, point blank, to go into the cabin and the boys were told off and ordered to clean it up immediately. So straight away I'd made three new enemies within minutes of my arrival. They were a strange lot and the only one who would talk to me was a masseuse who would set his alarm clock to go off in the middle of the night so he could wake up to write his dreams down. He was a really weird character and told me his kids communicated to him through his dreams. So imagine me, little Leighton from Bradford, trapped on this cruise ship with his bizarre spiritualist-type person. I just didn't know what to make of it all.

I was really unhappy and after four weeks a glamorous American holidaymaker spotted my glum face. She came up to me and said, 'What's wrong with you? You seem really unhappy.' I told her I was missing home and my family. She said, 'I want you to come out with me tonight. We'll go to the casino.' Her father was a rich businessman who had hired a whole deck for his entire company to go on a bonding cruise so she was one of our VIP passengers. I told the salon manager that I'd been invited to the casino but she said I wasn't allowed to go. It was the ship's rules that you couldn't socialise with the guests but she didn't stand a chance against this pushy guest. The guest calmly asked her, 'Do you want me to get a free cruise for everyone that my father has brought onto this ship because you're offending me right now!' She told her to get the captain and inform him who her father was. Being cocky as I was, I was determined to go on my night out even if it didn't do me any favours later down the line.

That night was incredible. We went to the casino, got drunk and she had me rolling the dice for her. She was playing with $5k chips! I'd never seen anything like it in my life, people throwing money around like that. I had the best time. We were dancing and having fun. I got in late and the b*stards I was sharing with didn't wake me up the next morning. I'd forgotten to set my alarm and woke up at 11.30am with the worst hangover. I was meant to be at work for 8am but no one had bothered to nudge me. I'd made complete enemies with the managers of the departments I worked for so they started to look at me a little closer and that's when they checked my passport – remember the forged passport from Kavos? I wasn't old enough to be working on the ships, as you had to be over 21. My passport said I was 23 but the truth was I was only 19. It was the perfect way for them to get rid of me so they reported me to Customs when the ship docked at one of its stops. They were really evil and nasty as I was only a little kid at the time and they knew nothing about me but they were behaving like I was a big time criminal. They said, 'We don't know if he's been smuggling drugs from somewhere or if his name is really Leighton Denny. It doesn't even sound like a real name.' They wanted me gone. Customs told them they'd have to deal with it back in Miami, as that's where I had boarded the ship. So I was confined to the cabin like a prisoner and only allowed to leave for one hour a day of daylight and even then I had to be escorted at all times. To make matters worse I was only allowed at the back of the ship where the clay pigeons were fired so I didn't have any contact with any other staff members or guests.

When the ship finally docked back in Miami, US Customs came on board and started shouting at me. A really mean looking guy had a looking glass and kept looking over my passport saying it was a fake. I tried to explain that I'd forged it in Kavos to hire a moped when I was 14 but they wouldn't listen to me. I'd used the new paper Tip Ex and changed the last digit of my birth date from 1974 to 1970, as it was a hand written passport. I was thumbcuffed, arrested and marched off the ship in front of all the passengers. They threw me into a Miami police cell with bars where I could see all the other criminals caged up. I was petrified. I had to stay there until the passport office opened at home as I'd been arrested on a bank holiday weekend in the UK. Thankfully, once they got through to the passport office in London they were able to confirm that my passport wasn't fake and I'd forged the dates.

They ordered me to be sent back to the UK on the first available flight home. What was really amusing is they only had First Class seats left so little Leighton flew back to London in cushy First Class – maybe that was a taste of the life to come. When I arrived back in the UK I couldn't face going back to Bradford and explaining to my parents what had happened. I'd made some friends in London by this stage so I ended up staying there for a few weeks just partying and crashing on people's sofas. I always loved London and always knew I'd end up living there but I wanted to make sure I was financially secure first. So many young kids moved to London and always seemed to fall into crime and prostitution, as it was so hard to survive in the city. I knew my big move was far away but when I did make the leap I'd do it properly and not get caught out like so many others had.

Funnily enough, I'd been to a psychic lady called Jane Crump who told me that I was destined for big things and would end up living in London one day. My cousin Jolene had been to see her just after her dad, Mad Dog Riley, had died. Jolene had got it into her head that if she went to see a psychic she may be able to speak to her dad. Jolene was stunned with the amount of things that Jane old her and found her absolutely unbelievable. I was a little sceptical about the whole thing so I went to see this woman mainly to check her out. Jane lived in a little council house in Tyersal, just around the corner from my salon in Bradford. She was a bit mental and her eyes went funny when she was doing the reading. It was a little bit scary at first until you got to know her. She had loads of dogs and animals around. Jane charged £20 and she told me she hated charging for it but she couldn't do other work because of her gift. She considered it a gift as people spoke to her and ran it as a proper business and paid tax. Jane would never take any more money and she wouldn't finish until she told you everything that had come through to her. From the moment I stepped in her door she knew I'd come in with a sceptical mind. She went, 'Ahhh you don't believe me, do you?'
Jane told me to choose different coloured ribbons – whichever ones I was drawn to – as that's how she was

able to read things. She immediately told me, 'Your life is going to be amazing. I can see you in Los Angeles. But before that, you're going to go to London and you're going to win loads of awards. I can see you on the stage and you've got a dickie bow on and you're all dressed up.' I was thinking, 'what's she on about?' Fast forward a few years later and I was picking up some industry awards at the British Beauty Awards. It was a black tie occasion, and what was I wearing? A dickie bow! Exactly what Jane Crump had predicted.

9. THE GREAT ESCAPE

I'd found myself trapped in another relationship with a girl called Suzy but I'd already started venturing out in the gay scene to a club called Vague. It was the first club night of its kind – really funky and mixed with both straights and gays. So, in my eyes, it was all right to go there as it wasn't just a gay club. It was run by TWA – Trannies With Attitude – who were actually two straight men who liked to drag up! They were really well known at the time and had a song out called Disco Biscuit. A little embarrassing fact about me is that there's a picture of me dressed up in a big, green furry hat and red lipstick (which they insisted I wear!) on one of the Vague CDs.

Vague was like a religion and we'd go every Saturday – without fail! TWA would tell us the theme for the next week at the end of the Saturday night and then we'd spend all week coordinating our outfits for the following week. They had really quirky themes and I remember them throwing a Vera Duckworth garden party one week. Vera Duckworth was a fictional character from Coronation Street. That night they laid grass on the floor and decorated the entire club with flowers – just like Vera's garden on the show. Another week, they threw a beach party and filled the club with sand. I remember wearing just a pair of little Speedos and carrying a bucket, spade and lilo to that one - the wilder the costume, the better.

As the club became more exclusive, it quickly became

THE place to go in Leeds and it was notoriously difficult to get in as clubbers would flock from all over for a piece of the action. It was crazy as people were coming from London in helicopters at one stage and they'd all descend on this huge club called The Warehouse where the magic happened. I didn't have any problems getting past the door whore, Madame Jojo, as we were friends and I'd do her nails every Saturday afternoon. Jojo was great. She used to let me and my mates in for free and we'd get the whole VIP treatment. Everyone wanted to come with me as we could always walk straight in and we never had to queue. As people were so desperate to get in, Jojo used to make straight men kiss each other in the queue, as you had to be gay-friendly before you were allowed in. It was a real no man's land – it was VAGUE!

I used to hang around with two sisters, Debbie and Karen Sparks, during that time and we'd always have a lot of fun. You could lose your inhibitions in Vague as it had a real 70's vibe. It was wild but, at the same time, it was a really safe environment. It was a really big turning point in my life as it made everything ok, even if I knew deep down it wasn't. I felt like I'd be accepted and no one cared if you were gay, straight or bisexual. Nutty James was the Lady Gaga of Vague and he would walk around with hardly any clothes on. He was a really weird character and openly gay.

This was my transition phase as all of a sudden it was ok to be different. Vague embraced that. The more different you were, the cooler you were. All of a sudden I didn't have to hide who I was and we were only in Leeds, which was just ten miles from Bradford.

I met the actress Kelly Hollis through Karen and Debbie, and we all became thick as thieves clubbing every weekend. We all just clicked and became great friends. It was dead funny when Kelly ended up in *Shameless* as she was living in a rented house in Beeston in Leeds when we met. To be honest, we were all kind of finding ourselves at that time as we were more focused on what we were going to be wearing that Saturday night than we were on our careers or whether we had any money to support it. Most Saturday nights, after Vague, we'd end up back at Kelly's house as she had her own place. We'd carry on drinking before falling asleep and waking up with massive hangovers the next morning. Kelly had a bit of a wild streak back then but she was an amazing mum to her daughter Fallon, who was always her first priority, and she always wanted the best for her. I remember Karen and I going to see Kelly's first play at the Playhouse in Leeds, which was her first step into acting. It was a similar character to the one she ended up playing in *Shameless*. But she's not that person anymore, just like I'm not the person I was back then. Now she's a respected actress in *Emmerdale*, she's a great mother and, like all of us, she's completely turned it around. I still keep in touch with her and she popped down to see me with her mum a couple of years ago when she was en route to the British Soap Awards in London one year.

But rewind 20 years and our entire lives revolved around Vague and people would only book their summer holiday when Vague wasn't on for a week. Nobody missed Vague – even if you were DY-ING! I went every single week without fail for about three years and that era completely changed my life. The last ever Vague was so emotional we were all in tears that night. The promoters had fallen out and set up two rival raves, but it didn't work. Just like when Geri Halliwell left Spice Girls and Robbie Williams left Take That. It's just never quite the same.

Once Vague was over, we all started going to Paradise Factory in Manchester. Back then, it was just at the bottom of Canal Street which was gay-friendly as opposed to the whole street like it is now. We quickly found that every town had its own variation of Vague but the clubbing scene was a lot seedier in Manchester. The drug scene had changed by then and Manchester had a lot more heavy drugs. The clubbers had moved on from happy e's to the hard stuff, like cocaine, and people had turned to things like prostitution to pay for it. The whole rave scene stopped being fun and it was around that time that I decided I wanted to leave it all behind.

One night, a fight broke out outside Mantos on Canal Street and my friend John got involved. I was holding our mate Clare back and I remember having an out-of-body experience thinking, 'Is this what my life is going to be?' I'd been out clubbing for nine years and there were still people who were at least ten years older than me who were still on the scene getting high. I couldn't believe they were still doing what the teenagers were doing. That was it. I got the urge to escape again. I remember telling Clare that she was 'too good for this' then I jumped in a cab and told her I was moving to London on Monday. She looked me dead in the eye and said, 'If you go, I'm coming.' Clare kept her word, sold her house and moved to London a year later.

I wasn't working at the time as I'd already sold my nail business in Tong Street for £20,000. As part of the terms of the sale, I signed a contract saying I wouldn't work in West Yorkshire, so this move came at the perfect time for me. I went home, slept off my hangover then got up bright and early on Monday morning. I put some stuff in a backpack, got the train to London and never came back. Just like that. I'd told my parents I was moving to London but they were used to me coming up with bright ideas and I'd always come back home. So when I told them I was moving to London, Mum screamed back down the stairs, 'Ok, see you Friday!'

To be fair to them, every Monday I had a new big idea. Just like the time I wanted to be a fashion designer but I figured I wouldn't need to go to college. I'd just buy a sewing machine and sew things together. The whole fashion designer idea lasted about three days!

But this time it was different and in 1998 I excitedly jumped on the train to King's Cross. I didn't have anyone in London so when I got to the big smoke, a couple of hours later, I wandered across the street from the station, found a bed and breakfast, and booked myself in for a week. I was determined to make it so I threw away my Pay As You Go and got a new mobile phone so no one could get hold of me to try and entice me back.

I didn't waste time trying to find a job. I'd set out every morning and start knocking on doors of businesses asking for work. I showed them pictures of the nails I'd done as I'd decided I would rent a room and work for myself. Eventually I found a salon off Goodge Street called McCausland and Peccary. One of them must have been Italian, I guess. I think it was McCausland who was a nice older guy. There was a little one that wasn't that nice at all. But they had a basement in their hair salon that was perfect so I invested a bit of money doing this room up for the next few weeks. I was so proud when I set up my little nail station and I was almost ready for work. But I quickly realised that this pair were pretending to be something they weren't. I had my suspicions that they didn't actually have their own range of products, but would pretend they did to their clients. One day I came in early and heard the little business partner bitching about me and complaining that I'd left early the day before. They were treating me like a member of staff but I didn't work for them. I'd agree to give them a percentage of the takings. They didn't realise I was in the next room listening. I knew then it wouldn't work out so I started packing up all my stuff. The nice guy came in and I told him I'd heard everything and I was leaving. So that was my dream over. I'd lasted all of three days in my first salon in London. I was devastated.

Then my fortune changed when I bumped into a friend from Leeds in Camden one day. Steven Woodhead had moved to London a few years earlier and was now a hairdresser in Saks hair salon in Golders Green. He said, 'Don't stay in that B&B. Why don't you come and stay with us. We've got a comfy sofa you can sleep on.' I moved to his flat share later that night. I was relieved to be around people I knew. By this time, I'd realised how lonely London could be. The first thing I did when I moved was put an advert in the Jewish Chronicle advertising my services and I got an incredible response. I did nails for loads of amazing and crazy people when I was freelance and sometimes it got a little weird.

Working for the Jewish clientele was a big eye opener especially when I visited their huge houses around Hyde Park and North London. I had lots of clients around that area and I have to tell you about Mrs Lee. She was really old and she wanted me to be an escort for her – not sexually, mind you! I swear she must have been 100 years old and she'd still have her nails done every single week without fail. Bless her, every time she phoned me to book an appointment it would take about 25 minutes as her speech was so slow and I think she was lonely so she wanted to talk. It was the first time I'd ever seen so many diamonds on one woman. A diamond broach, a diamond-encrusted umbrella handle, anything that could be adorned with diamonds was. She had long nail extensions and would always have bright metallic nail varnish. She lived in a massive apartment overlooking Hyde Park on the north side. I'd only been in London a few weeks so I was in shock at how amazing everything was. Every day at 12.30pm Mrs Lee went out for tea and did different activities. For a brief moment, I considered accompanying her out a few times as she was such an adorable old lady. It was definitely my brush with being an escort but sadly Mrs Lee got poorly so I didn't have to let her down gently after all.

Deep down, I was still hoping I might be able to get a job in the Saks hair salon where my friend worked. All the workers lived above the shop and I slept on a sofa in a big hallway that was a makeshift living room. Steven lived with a girl called Claire who was the beauty therapist at Saks. She was looking to leave as one of her clients had approached her about going into business together. Claire didn't feel confident to open her own salon but I'd run my own salon in Bradford and sold it on for a profit, so immediately said, 'I'll do it with you.' We met up with the client who wanted to set up the business and she turned out to be Elaine Elias from the Elias family, who ran the big chain of dry cleaners by the same name. They owned a house nearby and they had planning permission to turn it into a private health clinic. We agreed that Claire would leave Saks and take all the beauty clients and I would turn a room into a nail salon. The deal was done and we moved into this gorgeous £2million pound house in Temple Fortune. We named our new business VIP Beauty. We got a massive Jewish clientele as Elaine sent all her friends from the synagogue in and I got loads of wealthy clients as well as my usual freelance clients.

I got a big feature in the Jewish Chronicle and I was well on the road to success. I'd gone from charging £30 for a full set of nails to £90 for a full set. I was fully booked and only working half days in the salon and still doing freelance clients so I was making thousands of pounds a week. But the more successful I was becoming, the more the Elias's were coming down on me. I'd only been there for six months and they were demanding more money for rent and were asking for ridiculous amounts too. I felt trapped but realised I needed a way out quickly.

10. FACING THE FEAR

I've never been that confident about sexuality but once I moved to London it gave me the chance to reinvent myself and become the person I wanted to be. I really got into the clubbing scene and I used to go to a club night on a Sunday called DTPM – Don't Tell Prime Minister – which was a gay club that was straight-friendly. Mondays were usually my day off so we'd go to DTPM at The End in London's West End before it moved to the super club in Farringdon. It was a really cool club with friendly clientele and although there were a lot of drug takers during that time, I was never a big fan. Everyone was taking ecstasy and it was moving into cocaine, which was scary, as it was still a largely unknown drug.

I sort of went down the clubbing scene for a while but it didn't last very long before I realised it wasn't for me. I didn't want to be involved in all the drugs and the artificial conversation that comes with it. The people aren't real and what they're saying isn't genuine. They'd be your best friends on a Saturday night and then you'd never hear from them again. I always had people from up north to hang out with, like Claire, Paul and Marie. Paul and I had known each other from back home. He'd come to work for me so I was training him and we ended up socialising quite a lot. I always had someone from my past with me. Any friends I made in London were more colleagues and I never really tried to create friendships. I've never been a really big drinker and when I did dabble in drugs I was never a really big drug taker, it was more to see what all the fuss was about. I quickly realised I didn't like it. Unlike a lot of people, I knew my own mind and just needed to try something a few times to make my mind up about it. I've always known my limits. Certain things impressed some people but I was the complete opposite. While some thought it was great they'd be 45-year-olds in the club, I'd be horrified and knew I didn't want to turn into that person. But if you wanted to meet other gay people you had to go to those places. The only other option was the likes of the renowned gay club G.A.Y that played mainstream pop music like Kylie Minogue and Jason Donovan. There was no middle-of-the-road venue until The Shadow Lounge opened in Soho. We always used to go there and hang out with celebrities. You had to be a member to get in and it made clubbing exclusive. I never had a problem getting in as a journalist friend of mine, Caroline, was dating the manager at the time. I loved it at The Shadow Lounge because you had to make an effort and get dressed up. It was small and intimate and you'd spot the likes of TV personality Graham Norton and Elton John's partner David Furnish there. Those were the days when clubbing was really glamorous. I've not been clubbing in London for years as it's lost that edge, and clubbers look like they're going to the gym rather than a night out.

Being in London gave me a newfound confidence and when I spotted the advert for Mr Gay UK in one of the freebie gay magazines I decided to bite the bullet and enter. I went to the final in Leeds the year before, and it seemed like fun so I decided I'd enter. It was great timing as I was desperate to open a London salon so I thought it would be a good opportunity to get on TV as the show was going to be televised for the first time. I figured a little bit of PR for myself on the gay scene wouldn't do me any harm and there'd be celebrities there too so it would be good for networking. By this stage, my mum and dad had sort of accepted I was gay but I didn't want to rub it in their faces so I decided if I did get through to the final I'd have to literally get them out of the country. No pressure.

My cousin was the voice of reason. He told me I'd have a hard time getting through to the finals if I went to the London heats as I'd be going up against the body beautiful Brazilians. He'd done some research and said the best place to enter would be Hull – no disrespect to the people of Hull of course. Fast forward a few months and I arrived at a dingy little pub with a stage and 15 contestants getting ready backstage in a disabled toilet in Hull. Can you believe the glamour? I'd got my new Gemini tattoo for the heat but I was really nervous. I'd banked on it being a small contest but what I didn't bank on was all the other runners up from the different cities had turned up in Hull to try their chances again. I seriously thought my plan had backfired as I had even more competition, and once I saw the other guys I didn't think I stood a chance in hell.

It was all judged on the screams from the audience so I thought all I could do was give it my best shot. A lot of people were wearing revealing underwear but I just came out in a pair of tracksuit bottoms. At the time, my body was in really good condition and I had a six-pack so I didn't feel the need to strip down like the others. I'd been trying hard and went on a Marks & Spencer's fat free diet for weeks before the heats. The compere on the night was gay entrepreneur Terry George and when I took my t-shirt off backstage he said, 'Wow, you've got an amazing body. Why do you keep your body covered up?' I smiled and thought that was definitely a good sign.

All the contestants came out onto the stage and had a mini interview with a transvestite host. It was quite tacky, to be honest. When she asked me what I didn't like, as a joke, I said 'gay people' and the whole audience started laughing. I said it in a comical, not derogatory way and that really broke the ice. Then we walked down the little makeshift catwalk and did a pose, and the person who got the loudest audience cheers won. I couldn't believe it when I got the biggest cheer and that was my place in the final sealed. I was crowned Mr Hull. I was gobsmaked as I was up against some serious competition that night. You couldn't wipe the grin off my face when I posed with the big trophy for my official picture, but they swiped it back straight after as it was just a prop they used at all the heats. Charming! This photo was used in lots of gay magazines. It was just the start of my great PR as they labeled me 'Nail Technician by day, Male Technician by night'.

I was thrilled when I got a letter from Mr Gay UK to inform me that I had made it into the televised final. The final was in Leeds and all the finalists were put up in the Hilton Hotel for the three days leading up to the competition. We had interviews with the press – mainly the gay press and one national paper. We all had to be interviewed about what we'd do if we won the title of Mr Gay UK. I said, 'I'd like to set a good example so people understand that being gay isn't about being a door whore at clubs, or a prostitute'. Sadly, some of the former Mr

Gay UK's finalists had fallen into prostitution so I wanted to highlight the positive opportunities that could come out of the competition. The organisers didn't appear very pleased with my answers but I didn't care as I wanted young gay people to be inspired by the show. The following day we were doing a photo shoot in the swimming pool and I was shocked to see five guys naked in the showers with their bums out and soap running down their bottoms. I refused, point blank, to take my swimwear off and they made it clear that if I wanted to win, these were the things I'd have to do. I took a stand against it and explained in a civil manner that I hadn't entered just to strip off. They suggested I could get in the swimming pool with some Speedos and pull myself out so my trunks had an outline of my private parts, but I refused again. Thank heavens I did as I'd be mortified now if those pictures existed.

The organisers came to speak to me that night and told me I wasn't doing myself any favours by not participating in the shoots. I listened but I always stood by what I believed in and I wasn't about to let anyone ruin my chances of a decent career in the future. It had been a really fun experience and I was sharing a room with a friend called Sean Stone who had won the Sheffield heat. We'd play Geri Halliwell's *Look at Me* and *Mi Chico Latino* over and over again on loop when we were getting ready to go out. We were so masculine – not! All the other contestants were friendly enough. It was exciting as we were going to be on TV and, back in those days, it was hard to get on TV. Sean had been in the final before and told me that people would naturally get offers to do porn after doing the competition but I told him I wasn't interested in that sleazy side of it.

The day of the final arrived and I was so nervous. It was held in the massive Town & Country club – which is now the O2 Academy in Leeds – and Channel 5 were there installing TV cameras on huge arms. It was all so exciting. They were interviewing us backstage and they were pretending I was the inspiration behind the gay doll Billy. I must admit, I did look like the Billy doll so they had a bit of fun and interviewed me about my lookalike doll. We had three looks for the final – swimwear, fantasy wear and formal wear. I was kickboxing at the time so I wore my kick-boxing outfit for my fantasy wear. It was exciting running through the rehearsals that day. I remember cruise ship singer Jane McDonald – now of Loose Women fame – was there and told me I had 'great teeth'. Jane was so cool and made everyone feel relaxed. Actress Denise Welch was also one of the judges and she was great fun.

But disaster struck just minutes before the show was about to start and I was the first one due out on stage. I started hyperventilating backstage. It'd never happened in my life and I was breathing into a brown paper bag, desperately trying to catch my breath. I knew I had to pull it together, quickly, as everyone was waiting for the show to start so I swallowed my fear and went out to face the deafening screams of the audience. I did a little kickboxing routine of roundhouse kicks, a spin, then dropped to the floor and did some press-ups before disappearing back down the catwalk. I was so thrilled with the response I got and I knew I had a lot of support in the audience as my sister Amanda, my cousin Jolene and quite a few of my mates had come down. I was a bit gutted that I didn't make it into the final three, but I knew I faced quite a lot of competition from the other guys. After the event, we all piled back to the Hilton Hotel for the after-party. Denise and Jane came with us, and Denise actually ended up going behind the bar and pulling pints. She was great fun and was in very good spirits, if you catch my drift. I think deep down I was putting on a brave face but I was disappointed with the whole outcome so I ended up going to bed quite early.

True to my word, I sent my mum and dad on holiday before the final was televised a week later as I didn't want them to feel embarrassed about it. I hired the reception of Holmes Place gym in Temple Fortune and invited everyone who I'd met in London to come to the screening. We got nibbles and watched it together as it was such a big moment for me – my first ever TV appearance. I thought my mobile would never stop ringing from that moment onwards but the only time it rang was to go for a screen test which turned out to be a porn movie – just as Sean had said. Let's just say I made a sharp exit!

11. YOU ONLY FAIL WHEN YOU STOP TRYING TO SUCCEED

I thought the streets would be paved with gold in London but it was difficult in the beginning. I'd probably say they were coated more in sterling silver. It wasn't easy, but I'm a true believer that you get out of life what you put into it. I was quite homesick when I moved to London, but I was also enjoying my independence. I knew I didn't want to go back to Bradford so I was determined to make this new chapter work. Before I left for London, I'd heard about Nicky Clarke's success and how he'd branched out from being a hairdresser to owning his own brand and becoming a successful businessman. I thought that was going to be my calling for the nail industry, but I never expected to branch out into all the different areas of the beauty industry and overtake any expectations I had for myself.

But success didn't come overnight and after about a year of me being in London things still weren't going as well as I planned. I realised it was all about networking, meeting the right people and getting your face out there. Sometimes, when you're in London, it can be the most popular, bright, buzzing place in the world, and other times it can be so lonely. You can be in the middle of millions of people and at the same time feel so lonely. When I bumped into Rachel Bains, my friend from school, in the West End one night, it was nice to see a familiar face. She invited me to a party in Camden as she knew I didn't know many people in London so she thought it would be a good place to meet new friends.

That night I went along and it changed my life. The music was thumping and the crowd was heaving with people so I slowly made my way through everyone to get to the bar. Those were the days when you could smoke in clubs and I noticed a girl having a cigarette, or more importantly, I noticed her hands. She had really nice hands, a long nail bed and was the perfect canvas for me to create my work. I was looking for a nail model at the time, and I knew she'd be just perfect for me to enter competitions. I remember saying to her, 'Hello. It's really nice to meet you. Can I just see your hands for a minute? You've got really beautiful hands.' She said, 'Me hands? What about these?' and pushed her breasts together and thrust them into my face. From that moment, I just knew Harriet and I were going to be friends forever, and we still are today. I told her it wasn't a chat up line and I was actually looking for a hand model. There was a competition in Brighton in the next few weeks so I asked her if she would be my model and she agreed. We exchanged numbers and I said she'd get a gorgeous set of nails out of it, as I couldn't really afford to pay her. She said, 'Yeah that sounds cool, I'll give you call.' We ended up going to Brighton and that's when I won British Nail Technician of The Year for the first time after entering for a few years before. Finally, I'd won my first big award!

The Elias's were coming down on me and didn't like all the success so I'd confided in Harriet that they were giving me quite a bit of grief. She asked me what I wanted and I said, 'I really want to get a salon in Central London but I don't think I'll ever be able to afford one as it's such ridiculous money. But if I'm not in Central

London I won't be able to get the journalists to come down, and if I don't get the journalists then I don't get in the magazines and I won't get to where I want to go in life.' Harriet said she'd introduce me to her mum, Marianne, who had an office on Moxon Street in Marylebone and was really well connected. Next thing I knew, Marianne was on the phone and inviting me to dinner at her house. She knew I was missing home so she asked me what my favourite food and dessert was. I've always loved really simple things like pasta, tomato and basil, and I adore jam roly-poly and custard. She said, 'Lovely, you sound like my sort of guy.' I went round and she cooked my favourite dinner. I told her what I was looking for, and she said, 'Leave it with me and I'll speak to a few people'. A few days later, Harriet called me up. 'Mum says would you be interested in this old bridal shop on Moxon Street as it's been empty for a couple of years. It could be a good salon.' I couldn't believe it. It was like a dream come true, but deep down I knew in my heart that I wouldn't be able to afford the rent. Marianne got me the details of Howard de Walden, the main landlords who owned, managed and leased virtually the whole of Marylebone. This was before Marylebone became what it is now. There was no Waitrose and Marylebone High Street wasn't trendy. It was just a little run down area of Central London. Marianne arranged a meeting with them and acted as my agent and did most of the talking. She told them I would take on the shop as it had been empty for a few years but I'd need a rent-free period. I didn't have much money at the time so there was no way I could afford a four-storey building. I knew it would be thousands of pounds a month to rent and it was in ill repair – like the whole of Marylebone High Street at the time. Marianne said I was going to be massive personality and have a chain of salons across London – which was a bit of a white lie – and that I wanted this to be the flagship one but I would need a two year rent-free period. I couldn't believe it when they agreed. We looked around the shop and it was perfect. Then I saw a door and realised it led to a flat upstairs, which was brilliant, as I needed somewhere to live at the time. It was a gorgeous two-bed apartment that used to be a brothel! It had mirrors in the bathroom, gold mirrors in the bedroom and I saw flyers on the floor advertising the services they used to offer. How ironic that there'd be a brothel above a bridal shop of all places! By this time, it had become unbearable at VIP Beauty in Temple Fortune and the Elias's were really trying their best to make my life difficult. Thankfully I got a call about three weeks later to say they had agreed to a 12-month rent-free period – and that was that. I had a property and not only that but I had a property with a flat above it. I wasn't able to move into the flat straight away as it needed a lot of repairs, but I was desperate to get out of Temple Fortune as soon as possible. By a stroke of luck, Harriet knew someone around the corner from the salon who was renting a bedsit just to get a parking space, so I ended up renting the bedsit in Marylebone for £80 a week. I took my clients from Temple Fortune and went freelance while the lease was being sorted out for the shop.

By the time I got to Moxon Street, I only had about £5,000 left as I just didn't realise the cost of living in London was so expensive. I was living the Champagne lifestyle on a beer income. I was addicted to buying clothes and was spending stupid money on designer clothes. Every Saturday, I would go to Selfridges and buy a new expensive outfit. I felt like it was really important to have all the latest clothes. I'd convinced myself that if I had a new outfit I'd have a better night. That was the mentality I had back then, which thankfully I don't anymore and probably why I spend more time in my onesie these days.

My dad gave me some advice with the lease just in case everything didn't go to plan. It was a ten year lease and Dad made me add a get-out clause after three years in case things weren't working out. It was £2,000 a week rent, after the 12-month rent-free period, and for someone up north that sounds absolutely ridiculous so I can understand why my dad made me put the clause in. I got the property and lived in the bedsit around the corner from the salon. My dad came down with some workmen from Bradford and we spent four weeks renovating the first area of the salon. Then I was able start taking customers within a month. It was my dream come true and more, to tell you the truth. We whitewashed the walls and laid IKEA flooring in the flat so I could move in. So I had my flat, the salon and my Central London address. I have a lot to thank Harriet and Marianne Morris for as they gave me the break. I ran with it but they gave me the break that I needed and they're still very close to me today.

I decided to hire a PR to get me on the map and get me some press for my new salon. I had a client who was a really streetwise girl who helped me understand the importance of PR. Even after being involved in VIP Beauty, I still didn't understand how it all worked. I'd told her I liked to do it all myself, but she said with all my awards and newspaper clippings from up north, I needed to get some press in London. PR companies are a bit like dating agencies between the client who wants to be featured in the magazines and the editors who decide whether they will feature them. It's just an introduction agency and they make sure everything runs smoothly and the journalists get everything they need. Often, experts like me are working through the day and a journalist may need a quote quickly but I'm with a customer. My PR would have a bank of information that they could provide to suit whatever is required from the journalist. I had always been under the impression that journalists came out and looked for new talent, but I was so wrong. The first PR I hired was a lady called Stephanie and she completely ripped me off. She was the worst. I paid her a lot of money and got no press whatsoever. So it's no surprise that that experience left me a little burnt. Then a client of mine, Claudine de Groot, recommended a PR called Alex Silver. I'll never forget the day I met Alex. She had a Z3 Convertible, was wearing this huge fake fur coat and she pulled up on double yellow lines. Alex was like a whirlwind and said, 'I haven't got much time but this is what I can do for you.' She reeled off all her PR ideas and contacts and said how much it would cost me. Then, as she went to leave, she shouted, 'Ok, let me know, bye!' Before I knew it, she was back in her car and gone. She was so Ab Fab. I thought I'd give her a go as she'd definitely made an impression on me and, to be fair, she gave me lots of advice. She got me out there and got me great press in loads of magazines. We became the best of friends to the point of staying over at each other's houses.

Alex was incredible. She started booking in celebrities for appointments with me and invited Tara Newley to come in for a pedicure. She came in but, to be honest, I had no

idea who was she as we had lots of different celebrities coming through the salon at that time. Tara and I got on really well, and at the end of her pedicure I remember her saying, 'I'll have to get my mum to come in.' So I was like 'Yeah, that's great' and I didn't really give it a second thought. I thanked her for the recommendation and thought that was the end of it. Tara wrote me a great review, which is what celebrities do in exchange for free treatments. I told the PR that she'd enjoyed it and said she'd tell her mum about me. Then they broke the news to me – Tara's mum was Joan Collins! I LOVED Dynasty and used to watch it with my mum. I'll never forget that infamous fight between Alexis and Krystle. Mum and I sat watching it squeezing each other's hands because it was the most realistic fight we'd ever seen on telly. Oh. My. Gosh. I had no idea that Tara was the daughter of Joan Collins and actor Anthony Newley. True to her word, Tara recommended me to her mum and arranged for me to visit her for a treatment. It was a Sunday when I went to Joan's flat in the West End to give her a manicure and pedicure with my assistant Fareedah Abbar. I remember it like it was yesterday. I was really nervous and almost threw up in the street outside her flat. My stomach was filled with butterflies, as this was the first really big celebrity and Hollywood movie star that I'd ever done. I'd had a few celebrities prior to her like Eastenders actress Patsy Palmer, Meg Matthews and presenter Gabby Logan, but Joan was big time. I'll never forget it. I nervously pressed the button and a really posh voice came over the intercom: 'Hellooooooooo?'
'Hi Joan, it's Leighton Denny. I'm here to do your manicure and pedicure.' There was silence for a few seconds then she said, 'You're early! Please wait.' Then it just went quiet. We were only five minutes early but

those five minutes felt like the longest five minutes of my entire life.

When we were finally ushered inside, Joan was absolutely lovely and pleasant. We gave her a mani and pedi, and I ended up looking after her for a while. I went back to her flat a few times to do her nails and also did her backstage while she was doing a theatre show. She was really kind and invited my mum along to see her on stage. Mum was so excited about coming down to London and meeting Joan. We've still got the picture of us all backstage after the show.

With celebs, it's you scratch my back and I'll scratch yours. Once the backs have been scratched and you've got the notch and you've done them for events, do you really want to continue working for free?

It's a good investment to put in as 15 years later I'm still talking about it. Joan was a great celebrity start and her name really impressed people. In the media, Joan was now officially the client of Award Winning Nails by Leighton Denny, but she had previously been a client with the salon just a few streets away – Super Nails of Los Angeles - which was one of the first stand-alone nail salons at that time. Joan was one of their biggest clients so it was big news when I started doing her nails – especially as I was only within a mile radius. It also meant a lot of general customers from Super Nails of Los Angeles came to sniff me out too. And to think it was purely by accident as it was actually a recommendation from Tara.

12. THE SWEET SMELL OF SUCCESS

Nails were big news at that time and all the American style nail bar chains were launching in London: 10 Nail Bar, Scarlett Nail Bar and the New York Nail Company. They were meant to be coming over to revolutionise the nail industry in the UK but they've all gone into liquidation. I'd already identified that the American nail philosophy was not going work in the UK – well not in a premium market anyway. The philosophies were people crammed in, elbows knocking, and clients in and out like a production line. I knew the premium clients wouldn't accept that and I made sure I stayed away from that in my salon. I always had individual booths for people to sit in. Rather than marketing myself as this speedy, cheap nail bar, it was more about the premium service with me. I always did extra bits. I'd have a soothing candle burning and I'd offer different teas, and generally I would create a more relaxing atmosphere. Customers had to pay for the extras but they didn't object as it wasn't just about speed and they were able to enjoy the whole experience. I wanted my clients to have an enjoyable treatment in a calm environment.

My philosophy paid off, and all the journalists loved what I offered as much as my customers did. Alex was great at getting press opportunities and came up with the idea of me creating the world's most expensive manicure using really precious gems. I'd come up with the concept and she took it to the next level by getting it into the media. I remember I'd gone out and bought a load of fake gems to give it a go. Alex took some pictures of it and sent it out to the magazines. Susanna Cohen, the Beauty and Style Director at Marie Claire loved the idea and asked me to recreate it with real diamonds that they would get from posh jewellers David Morris. They got me diamonds, sapphires and rubies, and they gave me a four-page exclusive. The manicure was just breathtaking - and so it should be considering it cost £16,500! This was my very first feature, and it almost killed me waiting for it to hit the shelves. The shoot was done so far in advance that it took several months before I was able to see my feature in Marie Claire. I wasn't allowed to create the manicure for anyone else until it had been published so I just had to bide my time. I remember the excitement of buying Marie Claire when it hit the shelves. I grabbed a copy and went round to Tara Newley's house in Notting Hill where we celebrated with a bottle of Champagne. Alex's plan worked perfectly and as soon as the magazine came out all the beauty editors were queuing up to feature me. At the time, I had Kathy Phillips from Vogue, Camilla Kay from InStyle and Newby Hands from Harpers & Queen, which is now Harper's Bazaar, who were all regulars. But it was Susanna from Marie Claire who nabbed me first. It's funny how I always wanted to be a jeweller as a kid, and I found a way to incorporate jewels into my work later on in life.

It wasn't long before I had big features in The Sunday Times Style, Vogue and Harpers & Queen. They all came out within a space of a few weeks and suddenly I was all over the press. That was it. My phone didn't stop ringing. I had TV companies calling, and suddenly everyone wanted a piece of me. I thought, 'That's it, I've made it.' For about a year, I was inundated to the point of having to sadly turn down some publications. In the beginning, I'd call my mum straight away to tell her everything. I'd tell her all the newspapers or magazines I was in and she'd go to the end of the earth to get them – even if it was just a credit for a photo shoot. Mum always wanted to see everything. At some points, I was getting around 80-100 pieces of press a month! Around the time my first bit of reality TV, *St. Tropez Summer*, came out I was featured in all the glossy magazines, and that's why I was starting to get fuzzy about my direction in life.

After I did the first shoot with all the magazines they started to book me regularly for their session shoots. It was at one of those shoots that I met Nina Taylor who went on to become the supermodel of hand models. Nina's hands and nails were perfect, and I'd never seen anything like them in my life. Every nail was identical and I knew from that day on that I wanted to work with this girl as she had the best hands ever. I suppose it was like a designer wanting to work with a supermodel because I knew my work was always going to look the best on this canvas. Nina became my new right hand girl as Harriet had met her husband David and was pregnant with her first child so she wasn't available that often. To be fair, Nina was a professional hand model, and Harriet was just a girl with gorgeous hands – but I was always grateful to Harriet as I did win my first awards with her. Nina looked just like Princess Diana. She dressed really smartly and spoke very eloquently. She spoke so proper and I was still 'Leighton from Bradford' complete with my thick Yorkshire accent. I later had to slow down my speech and learn to pronounce words rather than abbreviate them and not say things like 'innit' as foreign customers found it hard to understand me. Some people actually thought I was foreign. Funnily enough, Nina was never the sort of person I thought I'd be friends with. The Marie Claire shoot was in a studio in South London and the theme was red. There were huge tins of red gloss paint that we dipped Nina's nails into. The shoot was amazing. We had to put Vaseline over her nails and all over her hands then dip her hands into the red paint. We went on to do the most incredible four page photo shoot, and a friendship was born.

I'd imagined Nina to be a little bit stuck up but she was really cool and I can't believe I'd got her so wrong. We were having a laugh and being a bit cheeky with one another. I really liked her. Nina and I would recommend each other for every job we got so we quickly became the 'It' team for nails on shoots and worked across big features, photo shoots and advertising campaigns. We basically had identical portfolios. Nina has gone on to be the supermodel of hand models with her hands being insured for £2 million. Nina then became my best friend. First and foremost it was a friendship. It was just a bonus that our careers merged so well together. A lot of people in the industry were jealous of our relationship as she would always specify she wanted to work with me so other session manicurists never got the opportunity to work with her and vice versa – other hand models couldn't get in with me as I would only work with Nina Taylor.

Life was good. The salon on Moxon Street was insane and I loved it. I had a six month waiting list, and that was with me doing a client every 45 minutes. I could do a full set of acrylic nails in pink and white in around 37-41 minutes. I would have people call me up begging for a full set but they didn't want to book with any of my nail technicians, only me. The girls working for me were really good but my clients wanted me, and they'd bribe me with all sorts until I gave in. All my clients were generally great, and I got so many gifts – one client even gave me a car! It was just a little blue hatchback, but she knew I didn't have one at the time so she said she had a spare one I could have. Other clients would emotionally blackmail me and spoil me with so many nice things. At Christmas, it was crazy as not only would the clients bring in gifts but the PR's from the brands would send me amazing presents too. Plus, the brands that were trying to snare me would send stuff too! I'd get at least 50 bottles of Champagne every Christmas – and the real expensive stuff too, not Moët & Chandon. I was also being bombarded with invites to personal parties of clients and celebrities at their homes where I would meet their friends who would want to book in with me.

I had everything from free holidays with clients, flight upgrades and free legal work, and I never wanted for anything. I always had a client that would sort me out. They were like a little network. I was so busy working six days a week for the first two years that I didn't even have time to have a holiday or take any time off. I'd clean the salon in the morning from 7am and worked until 9pm. I always had to work late but I didn't care as I had a flat above. I was trained to do waxing, facials and eyebrows so I ended up filling in when any of my other therapists were on holiday or off sick. Whenever I sent my staff on training I would make sure I went too so I had a broad understanding of the industry. I always knew that I needed that if I wanted to go off into different areas in beauty – like my Sun Believable self-tanning range, Lip

Dual Expert Make Up and my new fragrance Light & Dark. And it's not that I'm a Jack of all trades and master of none, like some people would like to think. It's all about diversifying and keeping it interesting. When I think back over my life so far, I was happiest when I was in Moxon Street. That was because I felt I had nothing to prove to myself anymore as it was always my dream to open a salon in Central London. I thought I would have accomplished that by the time I was 40 but I ended up doing it well before my 30th birthday. Now I've got over 1,000 salons stocking my ranges internationally. I've even got 20 salons in New Zealand, and I've never even been to New Zealand - it's crazy.

I'd hit the party circuit as I was getting invited to all the exclusive parties. I was getting invited to everything, as people wanted me there. And boy was I doing it. I was going to the opening of a fridge door! It was all new to me and I don't know if I was really enjoying it but I was running with it. I thought that's what you needed to do to get ahead and I was prepared to do it. I didn't know what you had to do to become well known and well respected. I'd won Nail Technician of The Year three times. I was the first nail technician to enter the Hall of Fame as I was banned from entering the competition after I'd won the title so many times. I was invited to become a judge, which I did for a few years. It was an experience I loved. I had companies like Marks & Spencer, Max Factor, Coty, Crabtree & Evelyn, Chanel and Dior paying me to endorse their products. If I did a photo shoot for a A-list magazine I would possibly get paid £80 for the day, which didn't even cover my expenses in London, but I could sell my credits for anything between £250-£1,000 depending on the publication. I had the likes of Dior paying me £3,000 to sit in Selfridges and do manicures all day using Dior products for a launch or event. Max Factor paid me £20,000 a year to use their nail polishes. Cutex paid me £20,000 a year to use their products. Everything I picked up and used to do manicures, I was paid to use. So not only was I having money thrown at me by wealthy clients and foreign princesses, but brands also paid me ridiculous amounts of money to use their tools, so I couldn't lose. That's when it became a natural process for me to start developing my own range. I realised I could endorse my own range rather than endorse others. All it took was a feature in a magazine and the products would be sold out in the shops too. But I wanted to make sure I was experienced and respected in the industry before I did so. I didn't want to be a manicurist that suddenly decided to bring out his own range so I built up my skills working in product and brand development. All my endorsements with multinational companies were to promote their products but I was gaining a lot of knowledge from them too. I was learning the ins and outs of how the product industry worked. Caroline Pycroft, who was the Head of PR & Marketing for Coty, was instrumental in me signing my first endorsement deal. It was for Coty's brand Cutex. My PR, Alex, felt the next natural step for my career would be for me to endorse products so she arranged for us to meet Caroline at Patisserie Valerie on Marylebone High Street, which was just around the corner from the salon. That meeting changed my life. I connected with Caroline immediately because she believed in me and made me believe in myself. Caroline gave me the confidence to step away from my nail station. I evolved from being just a celebrity manicurist to becoming more brand-aware. Caroline was incredibly supportive in my journey and she's become one of my closest friends. We're still very much in each other's lives and I'm forever grateful for her continued support. They say you should never mix business and pleasure but sometimes pleasure comes from business. Caroline opened that door for me and I ran away with the opportunity.

When the Cutex endorsement deal was up for renewal a year later, I had a brainwave that I could just change the name of the company and sign similar deals with other brands. I didn't even have a legal person but I was savvy enough to seek other endorsements and already had a template contract to work from. I ended up being endorsed by Cutex to use their nail polish removers and hand creams, I was endorsed by Marks & Spencer to use their base coats, nail files, nail buffers and nail clippers, I was endorsed by Max Factor to use their nail polishes and Crabtree & Evelyn to use their hand scrub and cuticle remover. Those five companies alone were paying me £100,000 a year for a total of 25 days work. It was just crazy and not only that, but they were also supplying me with stock for the salon so I had no costs of goods for the salon. I can admit now that I went away with the fairies and I completely believed my own hype. I didn't like the person I'd become. I kind of lost my feet and was caught up in the hype. All the press were saying I was untouchable, incredible and tipped for the top – and I actually started believing it. I'd got a little beyond myself as I was pushing my fees up too. But I soon came back to reality. I was doing high profile photo shoots and working with some big photographers and make up artists who behaved like that. Luckily, I decided I didn't want to be like them. It was like an out-of-body experience. I didn't like their attitude and the way they were out of touch with reality.

The more I thought about it, the more launching my own nail range made sense as journalists adored me and I had lots of friends in the media. I was doing around 15 interviews a day at one point – everyone from Vogue to Woman's Own. Yes, I was the man of the moment but I knew it wasn't going to always be like that. I had people on my tail, like ex-employees, but I wasn't going to rush it so it was another two years before I felt confident enough to launch my first brand: Leighton Denny Expert Nails.

13. MY ENCOUNTER WITH SIMON COWELL

The celebrities were coming thick and fast as I quickly became the go-to celebrity manicurist. I was introduced to PR guru Fran Cutler at a beauty event and she told me that she owned an agency called Two's Company. Fran brought all her celebrity friends and clients down to the event so I invited her to become one of my regular clients. I knew she was close to lots celebrities such as Patsy Palmer and Meg Matthews, but it was her best friend, Kate Moss, I'd secretly been after for years. I would do Fran's nails in all these incredible styles just so she could show Kate my work, but I didn't get to work with the supermodel. In a twist of fate, I got booked for a photo shoot called God Save McQueen for Harpers & Queen. The shoot was with the women that Brit designer Alexander McQueen found inspiring. They included Skin from Skunk Anansie, Vanessa Redgrave and Kate Moss. I was so excited as I'd always wanted to do Kate's nails and had been trying to get her for ages so it was ironic that I'd finally got her by just being booked for a job.

I did Skin's nails first although I had no idea who she was as I've never been a huge music fan. I only used to listen to Capital Radio so whatever they were plugging is what I liked at the time. Skin was wearing a gorgeous leather corset and posing with her hands on her bum, which was a great shot. She had amazing nails. Next, I did Vanessa Redgrave's nails. She later introduced me to her daughter, Natasha Richardson, who became a client for a while. The man himself – Alexander McQueen – was

115

there on the shoot but he never spoke to me. He had his own little section in the studio, which was off limits to everyone. Sadly, both Alexander and Natasha passed away a few years ago.

But the moment I'd been waiting for finally arrived when Kate walked in. She looked so beautiful with bouncy hair! I'll never forget as Kate asked whether she'd have to get her nails done, 'Are they going to be in the shot as I don't think I can be bothered to get them done.' My heart sank, as I was so close. I piped up that I could just give her a little file with a fresh nude pink. She perked up, looked at her hands and said, 'All right then.' Relief. I got to work straight away so she didn't have time to change her mind, and we got on really well. After I finished, I asked her if I could take a picture with her on my little disposable camera that I always packed in my kit. So after looking after Fran Cutler free of charge for a year, I ended up getting Kate Moss myself. Typical. It was funny, as the more I worked in the industry, the more I realized how fashion and beauty differed. Beauty people were more fun while fashion people generally take themselves way too seriously as most of them felt that they were creating art. Don't get me wrong, there is an element of that in the beauty industry as well but we're not as serious as fashion folk.

It's amusing to think I even caught the eye of Simon Cowell back then. I'd made some interesting new friends in London and one was a girl called Zara who lived around the corner from the salon in Moxon Street. She was a gogo dancer at Stringfellows and was desperate to be a popstar. Zara was really good fun. She had peroxide blonde hair, a great body and implants which made her perfect for Stringfellows. One day she popped in to do her nails and told me the talent agency she'd joined were looking for extras to be in a pop video and asked if I wanted to come along. It was £200 cash in hand for the day so I told her I was definitely in! We had no idea what the shoot was for but was told we'd find out the details once we arrived. The location was a spectacular church in London and we found out it was a video shoot for the new pop group Girl Thing.

Girl Thing were supposedly going to be the next Spice Girls, who were the biggest things in pop at the time. A pop mogul was launching Girl Thing to rival the Spices, and just like the original girls, they were five sassy girls with different personalities. All the extras were all dressed smartly in suits but they told us not to worry too much about our outfits as there'd be a food fight later on in the shoot. It was dead exciting as it was the video for the group's debut single, *Last One Standing*. Zara and I made sure we got ourselves right to the front of the church for the video shoot as we certainly didn't want to miss out on our big moment. Then it was lights, camera and action. Girl Thing came out and you could hear the buzz of excitement as the camera started rolling. I distinctly remember a guy saying, 'Simon, what do you think of this? Simon, what do you think of that?' And they kept continually asking this guy Simon for his opinion but I had no idea who this Simon man was. No surprises that years later I realised that it was SIMON COWELL. I remember him looking at the monitor and he said, 'Can you get the lesbian looking thing and the blonde girl to sit at the back as it doesn't look right.' That 'lesbian looking thing' he was talking about was ME! I was devastated and shaved my hair off as soon as I got home that night. I continued to shave it off for ages as I felt it made me look more like a boy, and I didn't want to look like a 'lesbian looking thing'. There's nothing wrong with looking like a lesbian but as a gay guy, you don't ever want to be referred to as a lesbian. Girl Thing were such lovely girls and they really thought it was going to be their big break, but it just never happened. It just goes to show you should have kept me at the front, Simon! If you look for the video on YouTube, you can still spot me in the opening sequence of *Last One Standing*. I'm sat in my 'relocated seat' at the back of the church and to the left. Looking back, I was probably the first person to receive a public critique from Mr Cowell, long before X Factor and Britain's Got Talent!

14. SCALES CAN ONLY DEFINE YOUR WEIGHT, NOT WHO YOU ARE

I needed a new body to go with my new life, but I knew that would be challenging as I've always battled with my weight and still do now. My little network of clients came in handy, again, as one of their husband's was a personal trainer called Bob so I was able to get a discount. For as long as I can remember, I have always loved my food. Fish and chips, and Sunday dinners were my absolute favourites. I didn't even know what a diet was! As a kid, I loved sweets and would easily spend my entire £5 pocket money buying bags of the stuff. I got fat but weight wasn't an issue in those days. I don't even think there was a gym in Bradford for crying out loud. If there was, it wouldn't be anything like Holmes Place. It would be a council-run sports centre with a swimming pool, if we were lucky. I have the same build as my dad, but he was always really fit as training the greyhounds kept him really active. I guess most people expect the puppy fat to drop off eventually, but it was only when I started going clubbing as a teenager that I became more body conscious.

My weight has yoyo-ed from 8st to 15st. I've had the perfect body with a six-pack, but it's only as I got older that I realised that it didn't make me happy – even though I thought that's what I needed to be happy at the time. The nightmare starts when you're trying to get that perfect body. I love carbohydrates and you can't get and keep a six-pack unless you've got it genetically. I love

Slimming World. That's my diet of choice as you can eat just carbs.

My obsession started when I found out I'd be doing a huge photo shoot for Gay Times. It was a big deal for me. I knew I had to be in the best shape of my life as it was a topless shoot. It sent me spiralling out of control, and I got completely obsessive about working out and losing weight. It was probably the closest I've ever had to having an eating disorder. I was a member of Holmes Place gym in Marylebone, and I actually got banned from the gym for doing too much cardio. I was doing two hours cardio before work. At lunchtime, I'd do an hour's personal training and then after work I'd do another two hours of cardio. And I was on Slimming World at the time. It was all for this bloody photo shoot. But the gym manager was clocking how much I was there and said he had no choice but to ban me from doing cardio as I was overdoing the recommended amount each day. I was allowed to do weights but not the excessive cardio. I got down to the lightest I've ever weighed. I was a tiny 8st, which is underweight for my 5ft 8in height. My body fat went down to 2.9 per cent. I was taking my health to a dangerous level. I felt like I had to be skinny. I was doing the Gay Times feature, going to St. Tropez to film the reality TV show and everywhere you looked it was all about being skinny. Geri Halliwell had left the Spice Girls and came back skinny. I felt like this was my time and my opportunity. Sadly, I failed to realise that it didn't actually matter what size I was. My only focus was to be this skinny new me.

I loved having a six-pack so I was getting it out at any opportunity. I'm cringing just thinking about it now. I'd

120

wear my shirts unbuttoned and the moment anyone commented that I'd lost weight I'd pull my t-shirt up and ask if they'd seen my six-pack. I'd never done a photo shoot where I was the model and I knew I would hardly be wearing any clothes so I wanted to look the best that I could. There was no airbrushing at that time and the shoot wasn't even digital. It was shot on film so there was no cheating. I had to look good! The shoot was amazing and shot by world-renowned fashion and beauty photographer Tony McGee. My friend Harriet came with me and there were two male models and another female model. The theme of the shoot was 'The Ultimate Hand Job' so all you could see was my half-naked body with several pairs of hands covering it. This was a real breakthrough for me as a nail technician had never been shot for Gay Times before. It was my chance to prove that I was more than just a nail technician and I was forging a real career for myself and determined to go places. I was even the first nail technician to be on the cover of Scratch magazine – which is the nail industry's bible. I was semi clad and really pushed the boundaries. I really believe that I created a platform for manicurists. No one endorsed brands like I did before and now every brand has a celebrity manicurist who works for them. I always wanted to be the first at everything I did. Unfortunately, as my profile was raising the backlash started and some industry people started to bad-mouth me. They felt that I was getting too big for my boots, but it wasn't their job to try and put me in my place. The haters should have focused on themselves and let me get on with what I wanted to do and that was changing the face of the nail industry one step at a time.

London was hard work but fun although I still got really homesick. I used to speak to my parents every single day. I would send Mum photographs of nails that I'd done or pictures of my mates and me on nights out. This was before the days of picture messaging but I used to have disposable cameras with me and I'd take them to be developed before sending the shots to my mum. She loved seeing all the celebrities I'd worked with too. I know my mum really missed me. She took it really badly when she realised that I wasn't coming back. Mum and Dad didn't come down that often but my sister and her husband would come and visit me. As we got older, our relationship definitely changed for the better. By the time I was 18, me and my sister didn't really have a close relationship but when I got my head down and started to concentrate on my career Amanda was there for me 100 per cent. She'd been hurt so much by Stephen's antics that when I started going clubbing she was frightened that I'd turn out the same way as him. Our Amanda always thought she was a cut above and she proved that she was. She's become really successful and she's never left Bradford. Amanda likes being a big fish in a little pond so while she never wanted to leave our hometown, I couldn't wait to escape. I didn't want to leave my family or Bradford and I feel in my heart I'll end up retiring there. I'd get really tearful sometimes, especially when Mum was poorly. She had a tough time going through the menopause as she struggled to find a hormone replacement therapy (HRT) treatment that worked. She got confused with some tablets and ended up taking too many sleeping tablets once. Mum was rushed to hospital as they had no idea whether she'd actually wake up. That was so hard as I was stuck in London and couldn't get back home fast enough. My dad didn't want me to panic so he didn't want to tell me but our Amanda called me straight away. It was awful as I'd been out partying so I couldn't just jump in the car and hit the M1. I got the first train out of King's Cross at 5.25am the next morning and it was the longest train journey of my life. But Mum's a fighter and she pulled through. At times like that I really regretted living in London. Also, I couldn't leave the business for any length of time so it upset me that I couldn't go back home as often as I would have liked to.

I was working all the hours I could to maintain my dream salon but unfortunately I'd forgotten about the three-year get out clause that my dad had encouraged me to put into the lease. By this time, I'd completely revamped the building and hired four nail technicians, two beauty therapists and two hairdressers. I was paying my rent each month and all my staff with no problems as I was fully booked, featured in all the magazines and we were on the map! I'll never forget the day when someone came in from Howard de Walden with a letter and told me if I needed to speak to anyone about it, there was a telephone number inside. It was busy in the salon that morning so I said 'thank you' and put it to the side for a day or so. When I opened it, I felt sick to the stomach. They'd used the get out clause that I'd asked to be included in the lease to let me know that they were taking the building back. I'd just used every penny I had to get the building up and running and it was amazingly perfect. I'd renovated the entire place, put new flooring down and the flat was beautiful as I was expecting to be there for at least ten years. I had a couple of endorsements coming in but my heart sank as I re-read the letter a few times. They offered me another building but it was in the same ill repair as the salon had once been in and, by this time, I'd ploughed all my savings into this one. I had no money left as I'd spent everything. I was skint and had three months to move out. Luckily, I'd rented out part of the hair salon and part of the beauty salon so that was easy to get rid of. Some of the staff were on temporary agreements so I gave them the opportunity to leave or to work until we officially closed. My friend Fareedah worked until the very last day and probably locked the salon door for the last time. She always stood by me and still works for me today as a trainer for Leighton Denny Expert Nails. Like Fareedah, when I was faced with losing the building my PR Alex stepped up to the plate and was an amazing friend. She came with me to Howard de Walden and looked at other premises with me. She went above and beyond any PR and proved to be a genuinely good friend. But then our relationship changed and I don't know what happened. I think we'd got too much into each other's lives and lines had been blurred. I'd looked at a few possible salons but I finally decided I was going to take the space in Michaeljohn salon – which was a luxury hair salon in Mayfair – but Alex didn't think it was a good idea. We both had terrible tempers and got into a screaming match in her Z3 as we were driving through Central London with the roof down. She thought I was jumping out of the chip pan into the fire, and I was under so much pressure that we ended up falling out. We did make up a few years later but it wasn't the same and then we lost touch. I'm sad about that as for both our faults she really helped me in my career and it turned out to be the wrong thing to go to Michaeljohn. She had been absolutely right, and I wish I'd have listened to Alex Silver. It was a big mistake – an absolute nightmare!

15. JADE JAGGER AND THE KEY TO IBIZA

I lost everything when I lost my Marylebone salon in Moxon Street but nobody knew and you definitely couldn't tell. I still had a Mercedes SLK – on credit, a Bond Street address, designer clothes, the lot, but I was at real rock bottom. I used to love Dsquared, John Paul Gaultier, and Dolce & Gabbana's diffusion line, D&G. Despite things not going my way, I managed to find a flat above Bond Street tube station. It was owned by the Peabody trust so it was like a council flat. It was in need of repair so they let me rent a one-bed flat for £1,000 a month and I got my dad down again to help me do it up. I made the living room into another bedroom and rented that out for £500 a month – so I only had to fork out £500 a month. I rented it out to my mate, Paul, from home so it worked out perfectly. It was all about keeping up appearances, and while I lived at the flat for a year, I signed endorsements with Crabtree & Evelyn and half a dozen other companies. I make things happen and I don't wait for things to come to me. No one's ever given me anything. I go out and do it for myself. I came to London to make it happen and that's exactly what I did. I'd had a setback in my career, but I was determined to build it back up again and make my salon in Michaeljohn a success.

My flatmate Paul started seeing a Cuban guy whilst he was living with me. He seemed like the nicest guy ever. He was really muscly and handsome and Paul was happy. A few weeks after Paul met him, I started getting these weird phone calls saying, 'I'm going to kill you.' I had an Xda mobile phone/pocket PC. It was like the iPhone of its time, with a touch screen, and it allowed me to get my emails to my phone. I never put two and two together but I'd go out with Paul and get 200-300 messages and missed calls on my mobile. It was this horrible voice saying things like, 'Did you enjoy yourself at Shadow Lounge as I was so close I almost hit you in the back of your head with a bottle.' I was working at Michaeljohn at the time, and I started suspecting everyone. It seemed like a bit of fun at first. I was joking to everyone that I had a stalker but then it started getting a little frightening. I'd be at work, nip outside for a cigarette, and by the time I got back in I'd get another message saying, 'Did you enjoy that cigarette, c*nt?' or 'I know where you park your car.' Then my car got scratched and a few days later I found my windscreen smashed in. It started getting too close to home. I went to the police who basically laughed in my face and said unless my life was in danger they couldn't do anything about it. They advised me to change my telephone number, but I couldn't as it was my business number and my lifeline in the industry – everyone had this number from beauty editors to advertising agencies.

It was especially frightening when I was coming back late from photo shoots. Bond Street sounds like a busy place but by 9.30pm it's deserted and the entrance to the flat was on a side road, which was quite dark. My residents' bay where I used to park was right next to a park with big bushes and I started hearing things and imagining things all the time.

Then Paul started getting the same calls. One time, his

boyfriend called straight after and Paul was telling him how awful it was. He was actually sympathising, saying it was disgusting and he couldn't believe someone was treating us both like that. Then something clicked in my head – it was him! This is a man who'd been staying over at our home and was part of our inner circle. I told Paul that it had to be him as it never happened when he was with us and the joke is, because he was such a big strong man, we wanted him with us more as we were getting frightened. The next time I got a nasty call I confronted the caller and told him I knew it was him. He hung up immediately but the stupid guy called Paul straight away and said the stalker had called him laughing as he was now the suspect.

Paul was stunned but finished with him. I told him he could never allow him back into the flat or our lives after all he'd put us through. The calls and messages stopped immediately and shortly after we heard he'd gone back to Cuba, as he'd found out we'd gone to the police. It was awful and I would always sympathise with anyone who's ever had a stalker as it completely turns your life upside down.

I put the whole stalking incident behind me to concentrate on resurrecting my career. I'd kept three technicians – Lindsey, Shreen and Kerry – who moved with me to Michaeljohn. I always wanted to be with the best and MJ had the royal crest as Lady Diana used to go there, so I felt it was a good career move for me. Two guys ran it. Michael was still there but John had moved on. There was also a guy called Frank and a woman called Carol who managed the hair salon. I got on really well with all of them to begin with but that relationship didn't last very long. We couldn't agree on anything. But I was determined to make it work, and they gave me the space. I installed all leather chairs and glass units just like I had before.

I went on a week's holiday once and I came back to find they'd painted my salon pink while I'd been away. They felt it was their salon even though it was a profit share. I owned a share of it. They took a percentage of the tills and paid the staff. They did have a fantastic PR guy called John Prothero working for them at the time, and he was brilliant. He got me some amazing pieces of press in different titles such The Telegraph and The Financial Times. Even though Alex Silver had been amazing, John took it on to the next level. But I just couldn't see eye to eye with Michael and Frank, and we were constantly at loggerheads. We had a verbal bust up in a meeting once and I just knew the relationship was dead. Things were definitely getting sticky and I'd not even been there a year.

Actually, thinking about it, it didn't work out at VIP Beauty, it didn't work out at McCausland and Peccary, and it didn't work out at Michaeljohn. The only common denominator is ME! I think I'm a bit of a control freak – actually I know I am. The thing is I've always been in charge of my destiny, and when people get involved and try and tell me something different – even if they're sometimes right – I just won't have it. I do not have to thank anybody for where I've got in my life, nobody but myself. There are people who gave me a step up but they usually got something out of it for themselves. There wasn't anyone that came in like the angel Gabriel and helped me.

Now Jade Jagger is someone who has been good to me from the day we met. We were on a photo shoot for Tatler around 2001. I used to meet a lot of celebs on shoots back then. At the time, she had recently been appointed Creative Director of Garrard – which happened to be right next door to Michaeljohn. She told me she had an office there so I told her that I was right next door and she should pop in and see me. A month went by and I didn't hear from her, then one morning I got to work and had a message saying Jade Jagger had popped in and would like to book an appointment with me. I saw her a couple of times and we'd really bonded, but the third time she came in I was quieter than normal, as I'd had some bad news. I'd just found out that my dad had cancer so I wasn't in the best of spirits when she came in for her appointment. Jade immediately picked up on this. She said, 'What's wrong? You don't seem yourself.' Being a professional, I shrugged it off and said everything was fine, but Jade wouldn't let it go. She said, 'Leighton, what's wrong? You are completely different to the last time I saw you.' I ended up telling her that I'd just found out that Dad had throat cancer. I'd just got back from home and found out it was level 4. Without any hesitation, Jade said, 'You need a break. I'm flying to Ibiza tonight, why don't you come with me? I've got a lovely flat in Ibiza Town that you can have for yourself. I've got a few friends coming out, and you need to come out and forget about life for a bit.'

Jade could tell from my whole persona that I was distracted, and it was nice of her to notice. I could see she genuinely cared. I said, 'Are you sure?' She was like 'Absolutely!' I thought 'You know what? I'm going to do it.' And I did. I couldn't get a flight that night but I flew out the next day. I called her when I arrived in Ibiza. She gave me the address of her favourite restaurant in Ibiza Town where she was having dinner, so I could join her. I got out of the taxi and was pulling my case down the port when Jade ran over, gave me a tight hug and grabbed my case from me. She was so warm and welcoming and introduced me to all her mates, including the tattoo guy who was the inspiration behind her skull jewellery. She gave me the keys to her apartment in Ibiza Town and I stayed out there for about five days. At the time, she was going out with a DJ guy called Dan Williams, and he got me on the guest list to all the clubs. I had some friends out in Ibiza at the time so it was brilliant. Jade was staying at her house outside Ibiza Town so I had the flat to myself. It was the most amazing flat by the side of the fort. It was such a surreal experience. Jade had this incredible BBQ for all her friends and invited me to join them at her house in the hills one night. I met her daughters Amber and CeCe when they were very little too. I had taken my kit with me as well so I did all their nails, as that was my way of saying thank you.

I'd been to Ibiza before but I'd not been with the Jade Jagger golden key, which meant I could go anywhere I wanted. I had a really good time and did forget about my troubles. I really needed a break. Jade did that for me and that created a special bond between us. I've since done Jade's nails for dozens of photo shoots, been to all her houses and we're still in touch. I love clients like Jade as she's not really into nails so I only hear from her maybe once every three months when she's got something on. Jade has a rainbow of different colours on her nails depending on what she's doing. If she's having her nails done personally she'll usually opt for a dark blue, grey or black nail varnish.

I love the fact that Jade always keeps in touch and has always been there for me. I've been involved with her on lots of different levels, and I was always pulled into her inner circle. I've been to her house parties, birthday parties, and lots of different events Jade's held. She was hosting a club night on my birthday one year and generously got me guest list for 25 of my friends! When she started doing her Jezebel jewellery line, she gave me a skull key chain and some skull rosary beads as a gift, which I absolutely love. Two years ago she made and designed these white gold and diamond skull earrings that I rarely take off. I've never charged Jade for doing her nails but she's been more than generous with me using her name, and I even blended some colours with her – Golden Girl and Diamond Diva – which are gold and silver tones and still top selling colours today. She named them, as her jewellery inspired these shades. With some celebrities you give, give, give and all they ever allow is for you to say you treat them – not that there's anything wrong with that as that's a very valuable thing. But then you meet people like Jade. At one point, I stopped saying I liked anything when she opened a store as she'd immediately ask if there was a sample or a spare one and give it to me. She's 100 per cent genuine and it's VERY hard to get into Jade's inner circle. Luckily for me, it happened in a very natural way and she knows she can trust me. Even if I became a billionaire, no matter what, I'd drop everything and still be Leighton Denny - nail technician – for her.

I had another regular client called Sandy McGee who

was really good to me and would always lend a listening ear. Her husband Tony was the photographer who shot me for Gay Times and my Scratch cover. Sandy invited me to her 50th birthday party at The Ritz and told me Leslie and Nicky Clarke were coming and she thought they'd be good contacts for me. That was just a bonus as I was already looking forward to going to her 50th anyway because she was a great client. Things hadn't been working out at Michaeljohn so I was looking for my next opportunity, which is interesting as things always have a habit of clicking into place for me. I'm at the point now that if something's going then it's time for it to go - it's quite exciting, and some things are meant to happen. I love looking forward to exciting new starts.

Sandy's party was fabulous and everyone came out to help her celebrate – even Lulu, who I ended up becoming friends with. As promised, Sandy introduced me to Leslie Clarke who instantly said she knew who I was and had some great ideas for me. I confided in her that I was hoping to get into products, and she totally filled my head with all these brilliant ideas. I was totally sold and thought it was too good to be true. She said, 'I've got all the contacts, a little black book, you won't have to worry about anything anymore.' Then her husband Nicky came along and she introduced me. He appeared to ignore her and said, 'So and so's over there' as he looked at my shoes and rolled his eyes slowly up my body until they met my face. Then he just shot me a look and turned his head in the other direction. She tried again but he just dismissed her and said, 'Leslie, let's move away.' He appeared to have taken an instant dislike to me for some bizarre reason. Perhaps he'd seen my biography where I'd said I'd seen the likes of Nicky

Clarke become a household name in shampoos so I'd stuck some stuff in a backpack and went to London to see what would happen. That quote had been picked up in the newspapers so maybe he felt a little bit threatened for some reason. Taking it on the chin, I had a wander around the gorgeous room and bumped into Ruby Hammer – except it wasn't her, it was actually her daughter Reena. She quickly corrected me and said she was mistaken for her mum all the time. She was with her father George Hammer and introduced me to him. George said, 'Lovely to meet you. I've got your name written down on a Post It in my office. I want to speak to you. I've heard about all these great things you've been doing at Michaeljohn. Do you want to come and do it at Harrods?' Can you believe it? I said I was definitely interested in moving and I was sure I could get my staff to come with me. After a few meetings with George, a deal was struck and that was it. I told Michaeljohn I wanted to walk away from the contract and they released me with no fuss at all as long as I left all my staff, clients and furniture behind. And I did, but after a few months most of my clients followed me to Harrods – especially once all the magazine features started coming out – as well as two members of staff from Michaeljohn.

16. WELCOME TO HARRODS

Leighton Denny at Urban Retreat at Harrods was just weeks away from launching, but as luck would have it I was suddenly struck down with a mystery illness. I had just signed the Urban Retreat contract and on the way back home from Harrods I had to ask the taxi to stop for me to be sick out of the door. I know, dead classy. That was the start of the illness, and I was down with it for a good three months. I couldn't get out of bed most days, let alone work.

I felt really run down and depressed after losing the salon so it's no surprise that I got really ill. It completely knocked me for six. I was in such a bad way that I ended up in hospital on a drip. I'd recently got back from holiday and at first they thought I'd caught a bug and sent me for tests at the Hospital for Tropical Diseases in Central London. I'd been so weak for a long time that my symptoms were baffling the doctors, but they eventually ruled out a tropical disease and diagnosed me with gastroenteritis.

In recent years I'd put myself under a lot of pressure to have the perfect body – especially when I found out I'd be spending that summer in St. Tropez to film the reality TV show. When I look back now, I can see that what I really needed was a jacket potato and a couple of roast dinners down me – with extra Yorkshire puddings! The sad thing is I maintained that ultra ripped body for two years but then my life changed dramatically. When I lost my salon on Moxon Street I also lost my body. Things were changing and I couldn't afford personal trainers anymore, as I was skint. All of a sudden I stopped dieting and exercising excessively and, naturally, I started gaining weight. My poor body was in turmoil as the minute I got ill I started losing weight again and got even skinnier as I lost a lot of muscle mass.

It was the wake up call I needed to stop my weight obsession. I realised that I needed to start building myself up. I quit smoking and ended up going the other way and ballooning to 12st. So I went from being dangerously underweight to being overweight. I was desperately unhappy especially as none of my designer clothes fit me anymore. When I was skinny I had to have all my clothes altered, as I was only a 26-27inch waist. I'd buy a 28inch waist – the smallest you could buy in the men's department – and have it altered. Nothing fit me anymore so I stopped socialising, which made me comfort eat even more. I would eat anything and everything. Unfortunately the entrance to the flat was next to the entrance to Bond Street's West One shopping centre where McDonald's is so I ate that virtually every day. I'm surprised I didn't get ill again. Without fail, I'd order a hamburger, chicken nuggets and fries every day. I was also a sucker for Zizzi Ristorante – a fabulous Italian chain – that did amazing Pizza Margherita and my favourite, tomato and basil pasta. I think I got caught in a cycle of binge eating but knew that I had to start cutting back especially as I was going to be working at Harrods soon.

It was a slow recovery but thankfully I got my life back on track and I was beginning to feel myself again by the time I started at Harrods. They gave me a tidy sum of money each month, but when I officially opened the endorsements continued to keep flooding in. I was launching things that had nothing to do with the beauty industry or me. It was launches, parties and Champagne soirees - just how you imagine it to be when you take up residence in one of the most prestigious establishments in London. Then the world's most expensive manicure hit the media again. Funnily enough, every four years it seems to come back round again. Two princesses in Dubai booked it. I flew out to the Middle East by private jet and it was pure luxury all the way. It was my first time on a private jet but I was taking it all in my stride and just enjoying the moment. I actually did the £16,500 manicure twice and created a £10,000 pedicure to match. I was carrying so many precious stones with me that I had a security guard accompany me on the private jet to protect the jewels.

My career was back on track and it meant I could afford a flat in Hans Place in Knightsbridge. I had the real address right behind Harrods, the ultimate salon location and the beauty know-how in my head so I was almost ready to make Leighton Denny Expert Nails happen – it was at the tip of my tongue.

I ended up working at Harrods for about three years and also had the Urban Retreat salon at Harvey Nichols in Manchester. I managed both salons, trained all the staff and worked in both booking in clients for a while. Now management tend to bring you in because of what you do and who you are but then, when you've achieved it, everyone starts to come in with their two pence worth. I started with nine staff at Harrods and when I left I had 19.

It was, without a doubt, THE place to get your nails done.

Wealthy women from all over the world would flock to Harrods. They loved how I did their nails so they would often fly me out to their homes abroad. I had two clients who insisted on flying me out to their homes in Monaco and Milan. They had read about me in Vogue, were real ladies who lunched and they liked the way I worked. They didn't think twice about booking me to fly out to treat them at home. I used to fly to Monaco once a month and once a week to Milan. They paid an absolute fortune. I was charging £100 for a manicure and these ladies would easily splash out £800 plus expenses for each trip! They didn't even think about it or blink an eyelid. But it's not like you imagine. Sadly, there was no chauffeur picking me up from the salon then helicopters and private jets. The reality was a cab to the airport, jumping on a budget airline and cab on the other side. I'd do the treatment and be back on my budget airline within a few hours. Oh the glamour! I'd actually spend more time travelling than I would doing the treatments.

I remember being booked last minute in London by some princesses who had just flown in from Saudi Arabia. The most expensive manicure in the world had become big beauty news around the globe and was picked up by The Fabulous Life of London, which was a documentary about our amazing city that aired in over 42 countries. I was the person of the moment in every magazine and every newspaper so was very much in demand by everyone. I got the call asking me to do the princesses nails as they were here for an event. I apologised and told them I no longer did freelance clients. It's no surprise they weren't taking no for an answer. Their assistant told me, 'Look, there are four of them and they really need to get their nails done tonight. Is there any way we could persuade you? I'll pay you double what you usually charge.' I really didn't want to do it so I made up a figure and said, 'Ok, £500 each.' They said, 'Great, when can you be here?' Within the hour, I was at their luxury apartment overlooking Hyde Park and did four full sets of nails – pink and white acrylics – and charged them £2,000. It was crazy but that was the sort of clientele that I had at that time. They wanted me and they were prepared to pay for me at whatever cost. And believe me, they didn't take no for an answer.

One of my favourite clients was a lady called Susan Olde who lived in a hotel in Knightsbridge. She had an entire floor just for her and her staff. Her wealthy husband had passed away and she jetted around the world staying at her various homes and favourite hotels. She would just have nail extensions with a bog standard manicure. I used to charge her £250 and sometimes she'd tip me £500. She was incredibly generous.

With wealthy clients practically throwing money at me, being profiled on TV around the world and having the most exclusive salon in London, it's no surprise I could feel myself losing my direction. With clients offering me £500 at the drop of a hat, I was making easy money without even trying. I had assistants at the time but the clients always wanted me so I drove my prices up because I was in demand.

So not only did I have my clients and day job, but I was also earning money as a session manicurist for the A-list publications. The more high profile I became, the less I was able to work with the lesser publications as there was a certain snobbery attached. If you worked exclusively with high profile glossies you weren't expected to work for the mainstream publications – which were seen as beneath you. I was always prepared to work with anyone who paid my fee but my agent wouldn't allow it so I found the ideal solution. My hand model Nina Taylor would usually be booked for the same job, so she would secretly get a taxi to my flat for me to do her nails before she headed off to the shoot. This kept everyone happy, and I didn't risk upsetting anyone or turning down work as Nina was able to work with everyone. Nina went on to be everyone from Kate Moss's hands in the Rimmel ad to Scarlet Johansson's so I was lucky to have met her when I did.

Working at Harrods had incredible perks and definitely opened me up to a new league of clients from celebrities to incredibly wealthy women. But as with every prestigious establishment, Harrods came with a lot of rules and regulations – which I was getting a bit sick of. I'd get last minute calls to do celebrities and would go into the salon to do them but days later would receive a letter saying it was inappropriate for me to wear jeans to treat clients. I'm a creative and you can't restrict me like that. If I wake up and want to wear tracksuit bottoms and vest that day, I have to wear that. I have to be me so if I feel like wearing a pair of ripped jeans one day I will and I don't care where I'm going. But I do know when to turn it on and dress smart when the occasion requires it.

With Harrods, I just felt like my job was done. It was coming to the end of my contract there, and they were changing the management of both Urban Retreats so I didn't feel like I wanted to do it anymore. There was no fall out or argument. It was the end of the year so it felt like the perfect time to move on. I'd been lucky to have a great team around me and, thanks to Harrods, I'd met my amazing friend Samantha Smith who was the Sales Manager of Urban Retreat. She is the most beautiful woman I'd ever met – with a pair of balls! Samantha was a former city trader with six brothers, so she was a ball breaker who was managing women for the first time – and 22 women to be precise. Samantha and I immediately struck up a great friendship, and after I left Harrods she came to work with me as a PA, confidante and sounding board. I was gutted when she left to go to drama school. Samantha's now a successful actress living in LA so things worked out for both of us. It's funny how life goes full circle as after losing contact for many years, a mutual friend, Sian Parry Jones, put us back in touch. Samantha and I now meet up for a coffee when I'm in LA. When I was in London, I'd have my northern friends and in LA, I have my southern friends. Samantha and I often reminisce about the good old days at Harrods. I don't regret leaving because it felt right especially as it was the end of the year and I like to begin the New Year with a fresh start.

I was contemplating my next year and what 2008 would hold and, just like that, I made the decision. I'd reached my potential and once I've done that I would rather move on to something new and exciting rather than get bored and lose interest. So as cushy and as comfortable as it was, I knew it was time to leave that life behind me and focus on my brand. It was the end of an era and the beginning of an exciting new one.

17. ADDING SPICE TO MY LIFE

I wouldn't really class any celebrities as close friends as my good friends have been in my life a long time so I wouldn't want to sound like I'm putting their level of friendship down, but I have enjoyed nice friendships with a few famous clients. I had a lovely relationship with Geri Halliwell. We met when she came in as a client in Harrods after reading about me in the press. Geri's so down to earth she actually personally phoned the store to book an appointment with me. It must have been fate as she'd always been my favourite Spice Girl.

I remember being absolutely gutted when she left the Spice Girls in 1998. I always had a soft spot for her as I've got a bit of red in my hair – well it was more strawberry blonde back then – so we both had a bit of ginger power going on. I'd watched *The Secret* DVD a few years before and it encourages you to create a vision board of all the things you want to happen in your life. I actually had a picture of Geri on my board, as it was my dream to meet her. The idea is you send your wishes out to the universe and they're supposed to materialise in time. I also had a Regent's Park 5-bedroomed house on there but that never materialised! But my Geri dream came true when I got a message saying, 'Geri Halliwell wants to meet you.' Geri had already left the group by this time and was doing well in her solo career – in fact, I did her nails for the last video she did for her *Passion* album. I always thought Geri was a fantastic showgirl, and she totally won me over when she performed *Bag It*

Up at the Brit Awards and came out of a giant pair of legs.

It was a really natural friendship between us. Geri was chatty and relaxed the first time she came to see me. We got on like a house on fire and really enjoyed each other's company. Geri visited me around a dozen times in Harrods prior to her going to LA – where she stayed awhile before coming back pregnant. Geri called me when she got back and asked if I could come and see her as she was doing an exclusive HELLO! magazine shoot about her pregnancy. At the time, she was living in George Michael's house in Central London so I started going to see her at home as she preferred the privacy. Geri loved to mix and match her nail colour. She tended to either go for very natural with nude tones or she would opt for a striking red or bright pink colour. I blended the Leighton Denny Expert Nail colour Sugar and Spice for her as she loved the nude candyfloss colour. Geri absolutely adores that colour, and it's still a shade that's on sale in my range.

By this stage, I'd moved away from doing clients and was only doing a handful of celebs with Geri being one of them. She has a nice tight network of people who she trusts, and I was privileged to be part of that. I was invited to Bluebell's christening and intimate Christmas parties at Geri's house, which were always really nice. I even ended up working on their comeback tour – The Return of the Spice Girls – and believe me, it was a dream come true. I was actually at Geri's house when she had the infamous summit meeting with Emma Bunton and Mel B. Mel had only had Angel a few weeks earlier and I just remember her looking absolutely stunning. She was glowing. Victoria Beckham was living in America and I don't recall Melanie C being there. It was so exciting for me as I was a huge fan of the Spice Girls. I was actually doing their nails as they were having the initial conversations about getting back together again. There had been lots of rumours in the press about the girls' much-anticipated reunion and here I was in the middle of the secret summit hearing it all unfold and how the logistics would work. The girls were genuinely so excited about getting back together again. It was just a question of working out all the diaries and actually making it happen. Things were completely different for them this time round as three of the band now had kids to juggle and Emma was pregnant at the summit. Geri was definitely the driving force behind the reunion. It didn't surprise me that she eventually made it happen.

It was a big accomplishment in my career, at the time, as I eventually got to work with them for the UK leg of the tour and went out to the 02 Arena - the huge state-of-the-art concert arena in South London – several times a week. It was such fun doing manicures for all five girls and matching their nails to their different stage looks. The buzz was incredible, and they loved being back on stage again. All the Spice Girls and everyone from the backstage 'glam squad' were great, and we all bonded really well together.

I didn't see much of Emma backstage as she'd just had a baby so was usually in her dressing room with him. But what I do remember is how high her heels were. One time, I popped into her dressing room and Louie Spence was in there walking around in Emma's heels trying to break them in for her – what a friend! I met Emma's partner, Jade Jones, a couple of times and he was a really nice, genuine guy.

I was never really a fan of Mel C in the early Spice Girl days – not that I didn't like her – but when I did eventually meet her properly I was blown away. She's such a sweet, pleasant lady who's actually really softly spoken and nothing like the aggressive Sporty Spice image we all knew. Her Roberto Cavalli designed stage outfit was by far my favourite out of all of the girls' outfits as it was just stunning. After the tour I'd say Mel C was actually the one that I got the most wrong as she's absolutely lovely. So the moral of the story is don't judge a book by its cover in the celeb world!

I'd met Victoria Beckham for the first time at Bluebell's christening. She's really, really down to earth and funny. Geri had recreated this fabulous Mad Hatter's tea party for the christening and hosted it in the garden. She had loads of cupcakes on colourful plates and it was a really relaxed, fun day. Then out of nowhere, opera singers started singing Wannabe. They'd been mingling amongst the guests then suddenly one of them started to sing, 'Tell me what you want, what you really, really want' in a really posh voice. Then all the opera singers suddenly popped up and started singing, catching all the guests by surprise. It was amazing, and to be in the presence of all the Spice Girls was incredible.

Geri had introduced me to Victoria and for some reason I felt a little nervous meeting her. She'd just had a new tattoo of Hebrew writing on the nape of her neck so I told her I really liked it. Victoria had already relocated to Los Angeles at this stage and couldn't help poking fun out of

146

my pink and white pinstriped shirt saying, 'That shirt is soooo LA.' It really broke the ice between us.

I met David Beckham backstage during the comeback tour when I was doing Victoria's nails in her dressing room. He is so polite, genuine and said hello to everyone. David and Victoria are both 100 per cent genuine, and I felt even more proud that they were British after meeting them. They deserve the success they have as they're a cool couple that look great together and they are family orientated and very humorous. Becks is also a lot taller than I expected and really softly spoken. I actually ended up working with Victoria on a few other projects after the tour. I did her nails for her and David's fragrance campaign, a TV ad and I even popped over to Beckingham Palace to see her. I remember her multi-tasking and signing lots of autographs with one hand while I was manicuring her other hand. She had very short acrylic nail extensions and she usually went for a classic natural-looking French manicure. Beckingham Palace was a real family home and the kids were playing in the pool and running in to see their mum every now and again. It just proved they were a normal every day family when they were in the privacy of their home, and it was clear that she absolutely adored the children.

I remember getting a text out of the blue one day from Mel B which said, 'Never change. Keep to your northern roots. Make sure this life never changes you!' We'd worked together on a couple of magazine shoots after the tour but it was nice of her to text me that. Obviously, I was closest to Geri out of all of them. It wasn't like being with a Spice Girl; it was like visiting a friend after a while.

I could always talk to Geri and she could talk to me. We confided in each other. But, the truth is, I never really felt like I was an equal as I was there to do a job in my professional capacity. I always made sure I kept it on that side, but Geri still keeps in touch by text and sends me Christmas cards every year.

It's funny how my closest celebrity relationships happen quite organically. Patsy Kensit and I used to share a mutual spray tanner, Moiya Saint, around this time and, just like Geri, one day she sent me a message saying she'd like me to do her nails as she had a few big work things coming up and she was also planning her wedding to DJ Jeremy Healy. Patsy and I hit if off straight away and got on really well. I actually ended up hanging out with her over the years. I'd go over to do her nails and we'd end up having dinner together. I was invited to her wedding to Jeremy, and I even went to Ibiza with her for her honeymoon. It wasn't like a traditional honeymoon as they'd hired a big house and they were there with family and friends so it wasn't a weird threesome or anything like that.

Patsy and I had got close before the wedding and continued to stay close, often speaking up to six times a day, after her shock split from Jeremy just months later. She was so upset and really thankful for me being there for her and, if anything, just as a sounding board to listen. Patsy was confused about Jeremy just upping and leaving so soon after the wedding and I don't think he ever gave her a valid reason either. I continued to see her personally and professionally for a little while. I did her nails every week when she appeared as one of the celebrity dancers on *Strictly Come Dancing*. She was quite nervous about doing the show but then Patsy always had a nervous approach to everything she did. She's not the most confident person in the world even though she puts on a brave front.

Patsy and I had got so close that we actually ended up going on holiday to luxurious health resort Chiva Som in Thailand. We were a right pair as I'd stopped smoking again and needed to lose weight, and Patsy was heartbroken as her marriage was over so fast. Embarrassingly, I was with Patsy the first time I was papped and they called me her new man in the Daily Mail – which was quite ironic. That photograph changed my life and forced me to do something about my weight, as I looked absolutely huge. It was definitely the wake up call I needed to get back in shape. That's why the Chiva Som was exactly what we both needed. It gave us a chance to really build on our friendship and just get away from the rat race of London.

I don't know what happened between Patsy and me but our relationship just seemed to change overnight. She invited me down to the 02 Arena to see her on the *Strictly Come Dancing* tour, we went for a drink afterwards but have only exchanged a couple texts over the last few years.

I really liked Patsy. We were very much in each other's lives. I knew everything about Patsy and Patsy knew everything about me. I think Patsy probably got a little bit nervous that I knew too much. We were even talking about going into business and doing my self-tanning brand Sun Believable together, which I eventually launched on my own. Things just fizzled out and it's sad, as we don't speak at all anymore. But it's like that with some celebrities. You'll go from being the flavour of the year where you're involved in everything and they ask your opinion on things in their life then one day it just stops.

I've never had to use celebrities in any other way than talk about their fingertips and I'd always like to keep it that way – I always swore that I'd never clip and tell.

18. THE GOOD, THE BAD AND THE DIVA

One celebrity client I absolutely adore is Dita Von Teese. She's by far the friendliest, most genuine, down to earth celebrity I've ever met. We met totally by accident as she was in Harrods looking at something and I spotted her incredible nails. She had the naked moon effect and I couldn't help but go over and tell her that they were 'amazing' and that I also did the same effect in my salon upstairs. She said, 'Really? I need someone in the UK who can do it for me. Can you do it for me now?' I said, 'Yeah, no problem. Just go to the reception and book yourself in to the Leighton Denny area.' I didn't tell her I was Leighton Denny, and I had no idea who she was either to be honest. I was sat at my nail station waiting for her and I was completely blown away when she walked in. I said, 'Wow, I really like your look.' We got talking and she told me she was a burlesque dancer. I didn't have a clue what that meant but she said, 'I'm like a stripper but I keep things covered up.' I did the moon effect with the white on her nails and she loved them. I remember saying to her, 'I'm really sorry that I don't know who you are,' but she was completely cool with it. She said she didn't know who I was 'so that makes two of us'. I gave her a little goody bag of stuff as we'd got on so well. A couple of hours later, a parcel arrived at Harrods and it was her signed book with a note that read, 'To Leighton, it was an absolute pleasure meeting you. I'd love to have my picture taken with you. Would you come to my Mac Viva Glam launch tonight? Will you call my agent and arrange to meet me?' I thought, 'Is this for real?' Panicking, my first thought was 'what am I going to wear?' I contacted her agent, Melissa, and she confirmed it all and said Dita wanted to have her picture taken with me on the red carpet. Red carpet? What do I wear? What do I do? I legged it home in a panic and ended up taking my PR to the event with me so she could liaise with Dita's agent. The next couple of hours were a blur and before I knew it we were arriving at the event. I wore a classic black designer suit with a matching black shirt. Dita's agent, Melissa, was lovely and told me that Dita was so thrilled to meet me earlier. I said I'd be honoured to work with her again and we exchanged mobile numbers. Then, as promised, I got ushered onto the red carpet and had a photograph taken with Dita. True to her word, she did all the pictures with the world's press and then it was my turn. There I was with Dita Von Teese's hand on my chest, posing for a picture. I was so petrified, and I looked it. It was one of my best nights ever. We went down to see the show and Dita came out dressed as a rhinestone cowgirl and got on a massive lipstick that was like a bucking bronco. That was it. A love affair was born for life.

Since then, I've worked with Dita for a number of shoots. She texts me and tweets me regularly, and uses all my products and genuinely likes them. Whenever I'm out in Los Angeles, we'll hook up for a cup of tea and a natter. Dita is the closest I've ever come to being a real friend with a celebrity, and I think we'll become even closer with time.

To be fair, I've worked with a number of celebrities over the years and I've never come across any negativity. There are always rumours that they're difficult to work with but they're not. It's usually the people around them who are hard work. The celebs often don't know half of the demands their management is making and they tend to be quite chilled...which brings me to my Mariah Carey experience - which I can only describe as odd!

It was my day off and my PR called me to say Mariah Carey needed her nails done. I'd met Mariah's PR, Connie Filippello, at Bluebell's christening, and she contacted my PR to say Mariah was coming into London and they needed me at Claridges Hotel in London's Mayfair in 45 minutes. Yes, that's right, 45 minutes. At the time, I was living in Knightsbridge so I threw some clothes on, grabbed my kit and jumped into my car. My kit was always at the side of the door, a bit like the 5th emergency service – that's after the Police, Ambulance, Fire Brigade and HM Coastguard. I didn't have time for nerves because I was too busy driving around in circles as it's murder trying to find a parking space in Central London. I ended up forking out for the valet service at Claridge's which I was not pleased about but, by this time, I didn't have a choice in the matter. Fans had started accumulating outside the hotel and Connie met me in reception to let me know that Mariah was running a little late. I assumed she meant half an hour or so but one hour went by, then two, then three! Connie kept coming back to apologise, but after I'd been waiting four hours I said, 'I'm really sorry Connie, it's my day off today and I haven't had one for weeks. Can I go away and come back?' 'No! Mariah's going to be coming down any minute now.' I was exhausted as I hadn't had a day off in almost a month so this couldn't have come at a worse time, but it was an amazing opportunity to do Mariah's nails. Then the big moment came and we were all ushered into a line to meet Mariah – there was a stylist, hairdresser, and make up artist, the works. Mariah entered the foyer looking every inch the perfect popstar just as she does in the pictures. I took my place in line but felt really out of place as everyone was dressed quite smartly and I stood there in a white t-shirt, a pair of ripped D&G jeans and some old Nike Air Max. Mariah came in and everyone was introduced to her individually as she walked down the line of people waiting to meet her. She was very nice and polite. When they introduced her to me they said, 'Leighton's here to do your nails.' She said, 'Oh ok. But I just want to get them buffed.' I said that wasn't a problem, and she was hustled off into her suite with a trail of people behind her.

I was eventually told to wait in another area. It was just frantic with people rushing around and trying to organise everything. By now I'd been there five hours despite being told to get there within 45 minutes! People were wheeling out lengths of fabric, rails full of dresses, carts full of shoes, and I thought I was obviously at the bottom of the pile. Then one of her entourage rushed out and said they'd been looking for me for ages and said, 'Can you hurry up as Mariah's waiting.' I felt like saying 'I've been here SIX hours!' But I just picked my kit up and sat on a grand throne to the entrance of her suite. I could hear Mariah on the telephone on the other side of the suite door. Her assistant told me she wanted her nails buffed but they'd need to see the buffer I'd be using. You couldn't make it up. I was being questioned by a complete stranger on what tools I'd be using. They didn't even realise I was using my own products and had actually developed this range. I swallowed my pride and was the consummate professional. I showed her a brand new trio buffer still in its packaging and she disappeared into the suite. The assistant came back and said Mariah wanted her nails buffed with an electric one and did I have one. I explained it was too damaging to nails and my buffer gave a really good finish. I even demonstrated on the PA's nails and she was impressed with the results. Off she went and the glass door was closed behind her yet again. I sat there for another 20 minutes and I had no idea what was going on, as I'd been there six and a half hours by this time. Then the PA came back, passed me the used buffer and said, 'Mariah doesn't need her nails doing anymore. Thanks for your time.' I just couldn't believe it. To this day, I still don't know what happened and that was the weirdest experience I've ever had with a celebrity. I still got paid but I would have preferred to have my day off. When I have a day off, I have a real day off. I put Sky Plus on, chill out in my dressing gown all day and veg out and eat bad things. Sometimes I don't even get in the shower!

Sometimes you inherit a celebrity client like I did with Nigella Lawson. I'd become friends with fellow nail technician, Andrea Fullerton from Hull, after we'd met at trade shows and had entered the same competitions over the years. Andrea was going on holiday and asked me whether I could see her client, Nigella, while she was away. I've always liked Nigella and jumped at the chance. She lived in a really grand three-storey house in the West End. When you walked in, there was a chaise lounge with a waxwork figure of a man sitting on it – which was really weird. But it was lovely to meet her and I was blown away at how gorgeous she was in the flesh. She's a really beautiful woman. She had a really big dinner table with loads of food on it. Nigella had me trying all the foods and the different types of dessert while the now infamous Grillo sisters were cooking. I soaked her nails off and did her a full set of pink and white acrylics. She told Andrea she really liked how I'd done them but I was too expensive, as I charging around £150 for a set at the time.

Davina McCall was a celebrity who left a really good impression on me despite the fact we only worked together once! But that's testament to her being a really decent person. I'd always been a fan and we ended up working on a photoshoot for Red magazine. She was styled as a magician's assistant and she was down to earth, friendly and really nice. She seemed really genuine and I remember asking her if I could take a picture with her. She was like, 'Of course you can. I'll get the photographer to take some pictures of us together.' I ended up on the set with her putting her arms around me and kissing me. Davina seemed really thankful for all her opportunities. I did shiny chrome silver false nails that were fitting for the theme of the photo shoot. I actually stuck them on with Blu Tack so we could pop them off at the end. We had a really nice conversation on the shoot. She asked me about myself, where I was from, if I had brothers or sisters. What you get with a lot of celebrities is they'll ask you a question but they wont listen to the answer. I found a lot of them have what I call a celebrity fever where they ask you lots of stuff but they have no interest in what you actually have to say. Davina was different as she looked in my eyes and was 100 per cent genuine. The way that she is on screen and how she was on *Big Brother* is exactly how she is in person. She was a real pleasure to work with her. I would have loved to have worked with her again, but it just never happened. But, then again, I've never really seen Davina have her nails done so perhaps it just wasn't her thing.

Now doing Dame Shirley Bassey's nails for a photo shoot for Sunday Times Style magazine was like an out-of-body experience. My mate Tony McGee shot it at his studio in Old Street. It was this huge gorgeous studio and everything was white - from the furniture to the walls. I remember everyone had to take their shoes off when we walked in. It was a really nice and relaxed shoot and we spent over two hours getting Dame Shirley ready. She was auctioning off a few of her amazing frocks for charity so the stylist was spoilt for choice. She had nice natural nails, and I painted them red. She was lovely, a really nice lady and we even posed for a picture afterwards too. I'll never forget this particular shoot as she went on set for a grand total of five minutes, then she said, 'Right, that's it!' She walked off set, changed her clothes and that was the shoot over with. Dame Shirley had left the building.

I've been fortunate enough to have looked after quite a few celebrities but there are only a few that I would still drop everything for. I've already mentioned Jade, and I'd do the same for Geri and Dita too as they just do a little bit above and beyond. It's not hard to be a genuine person after all. I find it easy to connect to people and can often connect to them on lots of different levels because of the life I've lived. But I found with Jade, Geri and Dita, it was easy to connect to them as they tried to connect to me on my levels as well. It's really nice and leaves a good impression. I've never had any problems working with celebrities, and I'd be honest if I had. It's nothing to do with confidentiality agreements or I'm frightened the celebrity won't work with me again. I've always been honest to the bone, and it's a trait that I'm proud to boast about.

19. DON'T FOLLOW YOUR DREAMS, CHASE THEM

The secret of my success is there is no secret. It's down to hard work and determination. Getting up early, going to bed late and not taking too much time off from your project until you've got it where you want it. I treat my new business products like children. New projects are just like babies that need to be fed and constantly nurtured. After a few years they start to grow, then walk and run themselves. Then you can leave them to go their own way like you do with kids. You get out what you put in. There was no quick fix reality TV or trust funds for me. I did it the good old fashioned way with hard graft. To me, success is about staying in the game in the long term. My first Vogue feature was in 1999 and 15 years later I'm still featured in Vogue. It's all about longevity. I've never been driven by money. If I don't enjoy it then I can't do it and if I don't believe in it, I can't sell it. That's always been my motto.

It's funny as I got a lot of confidence as I got older. If I could go back and give my younger self some advice I'd say, 'Knuckle down and work hard, don't listen to negative things' and I'd be a lot more confident. It was tough struggling with my sexuality and, at times, it was really isolating, as you know you're different from your family and friends. Being gay was considered something bad. It wasn't accepted like it is today. People were being bullied and attacked for being gay and I was already a bit different. Looking back, I would have definitely left home sooner as I realised that's what I needed to do. When I left for London I felt as though I could be who I wanted to be, and once I reinvented myself that's when everything started to happen for me. I had no hangers-on and no one to constantly remind me of where I'd come from or why was I different to my dad or my cousins. You don't realise when you're younger that people put you down as they don't want you to be better than them. You believe everything they say and take things to heart, which thankfully I don't anymore.

Now I'm focused on creating brands and making them a success. It's all about the thought process and building brands before moving on to the new things. I was Leighton Denny celebrity manicurist and I lived and breathed all things nails: acrylics, fibreglass nails, nail art, computer generated nail art, airbrushing and rhinestones. It was my passion but I evolved just like singers become songwriters and footballers become football managers. I realised I was still passionate about nails and still enjoyed getting my kit out and trying new technology, but now I love working on developing new products. I love creating things, the research and the competitor analysis. The public becomes my critic, and I love finding out what they think by putting it out on social media like Twitter and Facebook. Life's changed as you get instant feedback now whereas before you read what the journalists had to say. But now the public has a voice. Within 12 hours of my products hitting the shelves, I get instant feedback and they tell me where I've gone right or wrong and what they liked or didn't. I do feel lucky that I get it right more than wrong.

I've had losses and gains, but it's not about how you fall, it's about how you get back up. As long as you've learnt from the situation then it's invaluable as it's never going to happen to you again. I'm a true believer in that philosophy. When I went down I'd go down for a few weeks. My pride would be hurt, my tail would be between my legs but I'd sleep on it for awhile then I'd be back! I didn't wait for someone to rescue me. I made everything in my career happen for myself.

I was determined to launch a British brand for British women, as I never understood why we took the lead from American nail brands – especially as British women and American women are so different from schooling to lifestyle. My philosophy was bang on and that's why I worked at Michaeljohn, which had the royal crest, and then jumped ship to Harrods, which was the second most visited hot spot in London after Buckingham Palace. I knew that was the platform to anchor my philosophy and always wanted to strive for the best.

It was a huge decision launching my range as I knew it had to be right as I had a lot of people on my coat tails doing what I was doing, and I wanted to be the first at everything I did. I wanted it to be a true expert range so I put a lot of time and investment into developing it. I had started thinking about my own range years before it came out and was already creating bespoke colours for customers in my Marylebone salon where we had the clients' names on the bottle.

So, as soon I felt the time was right, I started to look for people to start manufacturing my brand. I knew what I wanted to do, what the public liked and what was missing from the industry. I always knew I wanted to be on QVC as I'd watched other nail brands on there that all seemed to follow the American philosophies. I'd done my research and saw what they were doing and the quality of their presentations and felt I could do it differently. There were so many things that I'd come across in my career and I'd always jot down the idea and put it in a big box. I knew exactly what I wanted. So I developed a small range for QVC. It was 30 colours, a crystal nail file, nail polish remover, hand cream, base coat and top coat. I had to include the core colours such as classic red and classic French because these sell all year round, then I could include limited edition colours inspired by the latest fashion trends. I would watch all the show reports from London Fashion Week that would give me the inspiration behind colours and different textures. I'd seen what was on QVC at the time and it wasn't very good so I developed a few kits and products that I knew would fly off the shelves. I was determined to make my range as unique as possible from the quality to the presentation. I've always loved Jo Malone. She inspired the presentation boxes that my products came packaged in. I liked the idea that everyone felt like they were receiving a gift – whether they were buying it for themselves or as a present. You should get excited from the moment you open the postal package, and Jo Malone packaging always made me feel a little special so I wanted my customers to feel special too.

I presented the range to four manufacturers and they all wanted to make it. It was about getting the right deal. I didn't want to spend one penny, but I wanted to own it. The deal I wanted was a royalty license agreement – which means you give the right to someone to produce something with your name and you take a percentage of sales. I also wanted to be the major shareholder so straight away two of the manufacturers lost interest and pulled out of the race, which left me with two to play against each other. In the end, there was only one manufacturer left in the running as I had been very clear that I wanted to launch on QVC and a couple of them hadn't supported that decision. To be honest, I got the one I wanted in the end and it was onwards and upward for me, as I knew this would be the moment I'd waited so long for. The wheels were finally in motion for Leighton Denny Expert Nails, which launched in June 2005.

20. LIGHTS, CAMERA AND QVC!

I was overcome with excitement at the prospect of presenting on QVC as I'd worked so hard to get to this point. I'd long got over my nerves from being on TV as I'd faced that fear head on years ago at Mr Gay UK. A lot of things in my life were about facing the fear, and I've never been afraid to do that. I had a school bully who was supposedly after me for whatever reason so I went to the house party I knew he was going to be at and confronted him that night. I would never hide and that came from my dad making me stand up for myself. He always taught me to fight back. If you face up to things they don't frighten you anymore and if they don't frighten you anymore it's not important. My dad explained to me that a situation is only ever as important as you want it to be and that's the best piece of advice anyone's ever given me. That's how I managed to block out a lot of bad things that had happened in my life as I refused to let them have a negative impact on me. More people need to realise that a lot of situations aren't that important, they're only important to you so you're fighting with yourself. You're creating your own animosity and you're in an argument with yourself most of the time.

I was determined to make my first show a success and for about a month before the big day I had all the collections lined up at home and flash boards with all the information on each product. I'd go through it each day so I had all the information memorised. I used to get all my friends round and pretend I was doing a live show. I wanted it to look natural and flow as smoothly as it could so I was determined to be well prepared. A couple of days before the live show I went to a screen test, which is a bit like an interview and run through. I met a lady called Tina who's now a really good friend of mine. She's someone who's continued to support me with all my new brands. She was the first person I met at QVC and it's her job to take you through the process so you have a successful first show. Tina was lovely and friendly and you could definitely tell she's used to people being quite nervous as she had a really calming vibe about her. I was there to do a mock up show called *The Guest of Excellence* with presenter Cathy Taylor. By this time, I'd gone in with all this information crammed into my head and it felt like if another word went in, I'd explode. I'd be cramming all the information in for days, as I was so desperate to get it right. I was absolutely petrified and had the most unbelievable sweat rings. Thankfully I was wearing a black shirt otherwise I would have been mortified. Tina was brilliant and reassuring. She said, 'I'm really excited about your first show, Leighton. You're going to be doing this on a different plane to what we've ever done before.' That really gave me a confidence boost and made me feel a little bit better. They explained about the monitors and cameras and taught me about listening to directions in my earpiece as the production team may ask me to wrap up the show or move on to another item.

In my screen test the production had said something in my ear and I answered them, as I had no idea you weren't meant to acknowledge them out loud. They wanted to see how I was with timing and said, "Ok Leighton, that's enough on that kit, "I piped up loudly,

"But I haven't finished yet! Never mind directing me, I ain't finished yet". Everybody started laughing – even the production team in my ear. They said, "You'll be great for QVC."

The products were my babies and I was just so proud to finally show everyone. This was the pinnacle of my new dream. Tina explained after, 'Unfortunately, Leighton, even though you may have more information to say about something, the products may have sold out so we have to move on to the next one.' She also gave me some feedback. She told me to use shine control paper on my face as it looked really shiny under the camera lights, lay off the fake tan and, most importantly, I needed to slow my speech down. She knew it was because I was excited but I was doing everything too fast. That was nerves and I still suffer from that today but it's genuine.

The screen test was a massive learning curve but I loved every minute of it – apart from my sweaty armpits. I'd rehearsed so hard. It would usually be about 45 minutes but as I did so much they called time after 10 minutes and gave me a Guest of Excellence certificate.

Two weeks later, my big moment finally arrived. I'd hardly slept the night before as I went over and over the presentations in my head. I wanted everything to be perfect. I arrived at the studio with suitcases and my outfit. I'd been asked not to wear black so I wore grey shirt and trousers from Reiss. My friend Paul came with me for support, as did my right hand woman Nina Taylor. I was going to show off and demonstrate the products on Nina's nails so we were both secretly little nervous wrecks. By this time, Nina was more integrated into my life and definitely part of my A-Team. Our relationship is a business marriage and a lifelong friendship. Nina's like a sister to me, and she would be the person I'd phone if I needed someone else's opinion. She was a brilliant sounding board when I was developing the brand and she's gone from hand model to working in product development with me. It's handy having a best friend who's a model who happens to have the perfect body, perfect legs and is a stunning looking girl. And I couldn't have coped without her by my side for my big QVC debut.

A former *This Morning* presenter called Alison Keenan was going to be hosting the Leighton Denny Expert Nails show with me, and I was thrilled. Alison had gorgeous nails and knew all about the industry so she was the perfect person for my launch show. I was backstage prepping and polishing the products so everything looked amazing and there was a real genuine buzz of excitement in the studio. I felt absolutely fine until they showed my pre-recorded promo and suddenly my face felt hot. I could feel myself burning up inside as nerves threatened to take over. By the time Alison gave me my big welcome I just about managed to whisper back 'Thank you.' In my head I was thinking, 'It's my big moment and I'm going to bloody lose it'. But as soon as my products came out I went into autopilot and started my demonstrations. When I got my first sell-out I thought 'wow'. I knew it would be a success and I was bang on. I launched nine collections and had nine sell-outs. I did 100 per cent more than my target. Every collection sold out. It got faster and faster and we ended up going into the reserve stock. We also ended up selling out of all back up stock as well and it took us 6 months to get back on air. I had amazing feedback from the first show. Tina had picked up that I was a little bit flustered in the beginning, but I'd pulled it back and was fantastic.

I knew I would do well on QVC and believed in myself but the manufacturers let me down a little, as they didn't have enough stock. It took nearly six months to get the stock together as they expected the stock to last two or three shows but we came off after 47 minutes and didn't even do the whole hour. They had to bring the next hour's show on early and it's never stopped, and this was before Facebook and Twitter. The only other place that had stock of it was my Urban Retreat salon at Harrods and by the next day the shelves were almost cleared. Mission accomplished. I called my mum after the show and she was crying down the phone saying how amazing it was. My sister Amanda called me and said, 'Oh my God Leighton, I was nearly sick watching you. It all went so fast. I had to take deep breaths.' Everyone knew I'd put my heart and soul into it, and it was the first time that anyone had seen my range. When I get to launch a product on QVC I may have been two years in development, perfecting the packaging and perfecting the formulas so this is the pinnacle for me.

When I win awards now, they're just as special as my first ones as it's still nice to be recognised for your hard work. I don't work 9-5pm, I work all the time. I even work when I'm asleep as I dream about projects and that's when ideas come to me. I'm the Creative Director of everything I do and I wouldn't have it any other way. I wouldn't put my name to anything that I wasn't 100 per cent involved in which is why I rarely take time off. Even when I'm meant to be on holiday in LA, I still work at least four hours every day as I can't switch off. I realise I have to be in charge of my own destiny and it never worked out at all the places I worked with in the past as they wanted to limit my creative ability. My babies are my products so I have to have full creative control. I'm more than happy for constructive criticism. I'm more than happy to listen to people's views although I may not take them on board. I have my vision and I always follow my gut instinct. When I was younger, I never followed my gut instinct and I've lived to regret it. I get a feeling and these days I know it's right. I'm a control freak but I've accepted that. I can live with that, and I don't think I've done that bad actually. You have to make things happen. I remember my aunty telling my cousin that she'd meet a rich man who would take her away from her miserable life – lets just say she never met that rich man! I always had the mentality that you should make a success of your life yourself and not wait for someone to come along and rescue you. I always knew it would be best to develop myself and learn from my mistakes. Something that could appear to be a mistake now could turn out to be the best thing that happened to you five years down the line – and I'm proof of that. Had my dad not encouraged me to put that get-out clause into Moxon Street I would probably still be there today. Had I not moved around so fast I probably wouldn't have moved into product development so fast either. Those disasters that happened are the reason I'm as successful I am today.

But success inevitably breeds contempt. You have to be careful as there are two types of people – people who are happy for you and people who want what you have! There's enough space for everyone in the industry, but people have wanted to take what I have achieved and put me down at every opportunity. I pity these people as its insecurities that make them behave like that. I'm secure in who I am, I believe in myself and know my worth so these people don't bother me in the slightest. Whenever I think back to the time in my life when I was truly happy it was when I was at my Marylebone salon in Moxon Street. I really miss it. That was my dream and everything I wanted. I wanted a Central London salon and it happened so fast and I fell on my feet. I was so happy and that's what made it a success as I was doing it for my true love of what I did and I wasn't trying to make loads of money.

Launching my first retail range for QVC was just the start of an incredible roller coaster journey as that was 10 years ago. Since then there's been so many twists and turns – more than I could have ever imagined. But that's the beauty of life: you never know what's just around the corner.

To be continued.

Made in the USA
Charleston, SC
16 August 2014